NOV
THE ORIG

NOVACOSM

THE ORIGINAL ZODIAC

Melissa Marshall
with an introduction by
Graham Phillips

Illustrations by Mark Marshall

ARROW

Melissa Marshall would like to thank Mark Booth, Lindsay Symons, Tracey Jennings, Mark Marshall, Caroline Wise and Steve Wilson for all their invaluable help

This edition published by Arrow Books Limited 1994

1 3 5 7 9 10 8 6 4 2

Copyright © 1994 Melissa Marshall

First published in the United Kingdom in 1994 by
Arrow Books Ltd
Random House UK Ltd, 20 Vauxhall Bridge Road,
London SW1V 2SA

Random House Australia (Pty) Limited
20 Alfred Street, Milsons Point, Sydney,
New South Wales 2061, Australia

Random House New Zealand Limited
18 Poland Road, Glenfield
Auckland 10, New Zealand

Random House South Africa (Pty) Limited
PO Box 337, Bergvlei, South Africa

Random House UK Limited Reg No 954009

A CIP catalogue record for this book
is available from the British Library

ISBN 0 09 954351 6

Typeset by SX Composing, Rayleigh, Essex
Printed and bound by Firmin-Didot (France),
Group Herissey. No d'impression : 28629.

CONTENTS

INTRODUCTION
Astrology: Science or Superstition?

THE zodiac signs are the twelve constellations, or patterns of stars, which fall in the band of sky through which the sun, moon and planets appear to move: Aries, Taurus, Gemini and so on. According to astrology, the positions of these heavenly bodies within the zodiac help shape our personalities and determine our destiny. Even today, in our complex, technological world, millions across the globe swear to the accuracy of their astrological birth sign, and just as many regularly consult their horoscopes in the morning papers. Are they all deluded? Or does astrology really work?

This century a number of research projects have been initiated to investigate astrology, many concluding that astrological birth charts prove far more accurate than should be expected by chance alone. Perhaps the most famous was the work of the French statistician Françoise Gauquelin, who in the 1930s examined the horoscopes of thousands of sportsmen, actors and scientists, concluding that their achievements had been influenced by their date of birth. Although Gauquelin's findings were initially criticized by other researchers, many, including the renowned psychologist Hans Eysenck, finally endorsed his results.

Most scientists, however, remain firmly sceptical.

Regardless of any statistical evidence which may support the case for astrology, the very idea that the stars can influence our daily lives seems completely contrary to the laws of physics. For most scientists, astrology continues to occupy the realms of magic and superstition.

But few astrologers consider themselves occultists or magicians. Some see their subject as an art, others as a science, but most believe that one day some natural explanation will be found to account for why, in their opinion, astrology really works.

Before considering the evidence for or against astrology, it is important to understand something about the nature of the universe: how the cosmos was envisaged in the past, during the birth and development of astrology, and how it is understood today, in our so-called age of scientific progress.

The Infinite Cosmos

Contrary to popular belief, ancient astronomers did not believe that the world was flat; certainly not from the time of the Greek mathematician Pythagoras in the sixth century BC. Pythagoras broke from contemporary thought by challenging the widely held theory that the earth was a huge disc floating on water. He advocated instead that it was a gigantic sphere. In a time centuries before the invention of space flight, how did he manage to get this right?

Pythagoras' reasoning concerned three observations: the disappearance of ships over the horizon, the shape of the earth's shadow on the moon, and the appearance of new stars in the night sky when travelling north or south around the curvature of the earth. Pythagoras, and others who arrived at the same conclusion, fell far short of the mark, however. They still believed that the earth was the centre of the universe. To them, not only the moon but also the sun and the planets orbited the earth.

Three centuries after Pythagoras, someone did suggest the correct answer. Aristarchus of Samos, in the third century BC, shocked the ancient world when he announced that the earth went around the sun. Unfortunately, unlike Pythagoras, he was not taken seriously. Although the argument continued, during the second century AD the Egyptian geographer Ptolemy finally established the theory that was to become the accepted textbook model of the universe for the following twelve centuries: the notion that the earth was fixed at the centre of the universe and everything else circled around it.

To both the ancient astronomer and astrologer alike, the universe was a vast hollow sphere on which the stars were fixed. Some believed that the stars were divine beings, while others saw them as distant windows, through which shone the light of heaven beyond. Called the *firmament*, this huge sphere was thought to rotate, with the stationary earth at its centre.

The stars of the firmament seemed to move around the earth, but remained in fixed positions relative to one another. Five bright, star-like objects, however, did not appear to be attached to the firmament. Instead, they seemed to wander at will over the backdrop of stars. They were called planets, from a Greek word meaning literally to wander. There were five visible planets: Mercury, Venus, Mars, Jupiter and Saturn, which together with the sun and moon (which also moved amongst the stars) were thought to lie between the earth and the firmament.

To some, the sun, moon and planets were the gods themselves. To others, they were great lights on seven transparent concentric spheres. Later, the Romans firmly established the importance of the planets in daily life, naming after them the days of the week: Saturday was Saturn's day, Sunday was the sun's day, and Monday was the day of the moon.

The modern conception of the solar system did not emerge until the early sixteenth century, heralded by Nicolaus Copernicus (1473–1543). Born in Poland, Copernicus was the first to seriously challenge the long-standing theories of Ptolemy. Copernicus concluded that both the earth and the planets moved around the sun, and that the reason it appears the other way around is that the earth itself revolves once every twenty-four hours. The majority of astronomers refused to accept the Copernicus theory, and it was not until the time of Galileo, a century later, that his ideas were finally accepted.

Although Copernicus was wrong in his assumption that the sun itself was the fixed central point of the universe, he identified the primary notion of misunderstanding the movements of the heavenly bodies by establishing the difference between apparent and relative motions. In other words, from the viewpoint of someone standing on the rotating earth, the sun appears to be moving around the world. Also, from the viewpoint of the earthling, the sun appears to move slowly across the stars during the course of the year. In reality, the sun is not moving around the zodiac, the earth is moving slowly around the sun. Consequently, the stars behind the sun seem to move.

Once this principle was understood, it threw a completely new light on the astronomer's view of the universe. It was gradually accepted that the human race lived on a planet that was itself moving through space, and once every year it orbited the sun. The next question to be answered, however, was why this should happen at all. Why did the earth and the other planets continuously orbit the sun? The answer involved the principles of gravity discovered by Isaac Newton in the late seventeenth century.

Newton's Law of Gravity states that every object in the universe attracts every other object. The more massive the objects or the closer together, the greater the attraction. Thus the earth exerts its greater gravitational force on a ball by making it fall to the ground if it is thrown.

This same principle applies to the earth itself, in that it is attracted to the greater mass of the sun. However, in this case, the momentum of the earth through space counteracts the sun's pull. In other words, when the planet formed, billions of years ago, the earth was too close to the sun to escape its gravity, but was moving fast enough through space to prevent it from moving towards the sun. It is therefore forced to orbit the sun at approximately the same distance for ever, neither able to move towards nor pull away from the sun's attraction.

When we stand at any point on the earth's surface and look up into the night sky we see a myriad of twinkling stars. In order to chart the heavens, astronomers require more than just the twelve signs of the zodiac to distinguish one part of the sky from another. There are in fact 88 constellations, constructed from patterns of the brightest visible stars. The constellations lend their names to the 88 areas into which the sky is divided for the purposes of identifying and charting celestial objects. Any heavenly body – stars, galaxies, comets, asteroids, planets and whatever else may be out there – fall somewhere within this constellation sky map. With so many constellations, it might seem puzzling that the sun, moon and all the planets only appear to move within the band of the twelve signs of the zodiac. The reason is that the planets are all on virtually the same orbital plane around the sun, and the moon – although orbiting the earth – moves through roughly the same plane. In astronomical terms this plane is called the ecliptic, and the zodiac covers a zone some 8.5 degrees to either side.

One of the main reasons that Copernicus' rotating earth theory was not believed, was that it failed to account for the fact that the zodiac itself moved up and down in the course of the year. Copernicus taught that the firmament, the backdrop of stars, occupied a fixed position in space, although it appeared to revolve because the earth itself was rotating. His opponents argued that even if this was true, the firmament still moved; during summer it tilted in one direction and during the winter it tilted in the other. The true reason for this apparent motion of the stars, is that the earth's axis is tilted towards the sun at an angle of 23.5 degrees.

The ancient astronomers were accurate in one respect; the moon does orbit the earth. The moon is much smaller than the earth, with a diameter of some 2,160 miles compared to earth's 7,900 miles. It orbits the earth at a distance of 238,860 miles, once every 27 days. This may seem strange, considering that there is a new moon approximately every 29½ days. The reason is that the earth itself is orbiting the sun. In the 27 days it has taken for the moon to go around the earth, the earth has moved further along in its orbit around the sun. It therefore takes about 2½ days for the moon to catch up and be back in line with the sun.

Earth is not the only planet to have moons. For instance, Mars has two and Jupiter has twelve. Others, such as Mercury and Venus, have none. One thing that the planets do have in common is that they are all in orbit around the sun; collectively called the solar system.

Essentially the sun is a gigantic mass of compressed gases, continuously burning in an ongoing series of nuclear reactions. It is approximately 865,000 miles in diameter, around 109 times bigger than the earth; its huge size is matched only by its searing heat, some 20,000,000 degrees centigrade at the centre, and 6,000 degrees at the surface. The heart of the solar system, the sun plays host to the orbiting planets and their moons, thousands of asteroids and hundreds of icy comets. As far as we know there are nine planets. Nearest to the sun is Mercury, followed by Venus and then the earth. Further out come Mars, Jupiter and Saturn. All these are visible with the naked eye and were known to the ancients. In recent centuries three further planets have been discovered in the outer reaches of the solar system: Uranus, discovered in 1781, Neptune in 1846 and Pluto in 1930.

The Romans thought that the planets were gods and their names are still used today. In reality the planets are roughly spherical satellites like the earth. Unfortunately, they are nowhere near as hospitable. Mercury, the one-time messenger of the gods, is airless and waterless, baked on one side and frozen on the other. Venus, once the Roman goddess of love, is a hell-hole, with searing, oven-hot temperatures and a corrosive atmosphere of vaporous sulphuric acid. On these worlds no life form conceivable to earthlings could possibly survive. The others are no better. Pluto, at the edge of the solar system, is a moon-like rock, frozen and dark. Jupiter, Saturn, Uranus and Neptune probably have no solid surface at all, being composed mainly of hydrogen and helium, so cold that they are in deadly liquid form. Of all the planets, only Mars is in any way earth-like. Sadly, if life ever existed there it is now too cold, with a carbon dioxide atmosphere and no trace of organic molecules.

Beyond the solar system, out past the orbit of Pluto, is the vast vacuum of space, beyond which lies the stars. The ancient Babylonians once believed that they could reach the stars if only they could build a tower high enough. According to the Bible they tried by constructing the Tower of Babel. We are told that God, concerned that they might succeed, intervened to prevent its completion. He had no reason to worry; the distance to the stars is far, far greater than the Babylonians could ever have imagined.

It may not be possible at this time to say how big the universe actually is, but what *is* known is almost beyond comprehension. To start with, just consider the solar system:

Mercury, the nearest planet to the sun, orbits it at a distance of approximately 36 million miles. Next comes Venus at 67 million miles. Earth is 93 million miles from the sun, and Mars is 142 million miles. Between the orbits of Mars and Jupiter, which lies 483 million miles from the sun, extends a band of asteroids, over 40,000 chunks of rock, the largest being 480 miles in diameter. After Jupiter comes the ringed giant Saturn, 886 million miles from the sun, followed by Uranus at 1,783 million miles, Neptune at 2,793 million miles, and Pluto at a staggering 3,666 million miles. Pluto is so far away that it takes 250 years to orbit the sun, as opposed to Mercury's 88 days. Mercury is also the smallest planet with a diameter of only 3,000 miles. The largest, on the other hand, is Jupiter with a diameter of 89,000 miles – 11 times the diameter of the earth. The earth itself is around the size of Venus and twice the size of Mars.

Perhaps it is easier to envisage these vast sizes and distances in the form of a scale model. Imagine that the sun is a ball six inches in diameter. On this scale Mercury would be about 20 feet from the sun, and Venus 39 feet. The earth, a mere eighteenth of an inch in diameter, would be 54 feet from the sun. Mars would be 82 feet from the sun, Jupiter 280 feet, Saturn 513 feet, Uranus 1,013 feet, Neptune 1,618 feet and finally Pluto would be about 2,124 feet away. This is almost half a mile away from the tiny six-inch sun. Remember, in reality, the sun is almost 900,000 miles in diameter. Of all the heavenly bodies, mankind has so far only stepped foot on the moon. On our scale model this would be a journey of less than two inches. These distances may seem enormous, but compared to the rest of the universe they are trifling. The nearest star to earth is Proxima Centauri – on our scale model it would have to be placed over 4,500 miles away.

The stars we see in the skies, once thought to be windows into heaven, are in fact millions of suns, many no doubt having solar systems like our own. However, they are not all yellow; some are red and others white. The size of stars also varies, ranging from small ones, about the size of the earth, up to massive balls of light, many times the size of our sun. On our scale model, with the sun just six inches wide, some of the giant stars would be over 250 feet in diameter. Although Pluto, on the edge of the solar system, is over three billion miles from us, the nearest star is 30 trillion miles away (30,000,000,000,000). At today's rocket speeds the trip would take 100,000 years. Incredibly enough, that's close, since most of the stars in our galaxy are thousands of times more distant.

Both the sun and our next-door-neighbour, Proxima Centauri, are in the great cluster of stars called the

Milky Way, a galaxy containing over 100 billion stars. The Milky Way, in the shape of an enormous spiral, rotates slowly in space, with its luminous arms trailing like an enormous Catherine wheel. The sun, located in one of the spiral arms, revolves around the galactic core once every 250 million years. Yet the Milky Way is only one of billions of such galaxies, scattered around the universe with vast empty space between.

Although not all galaxies are rotating spirals – some are spherical and others have irregular shapes – many are like our own. The average size of a galaxy is about 600,000 trillion miles wide (600,000,000,000,000,000), with the average distance from one galaxy to another being 20 million trillion miles (20,000,000,000,000,000,000). In order to avoid writing such awkwardly large numbers, astronomers use a unit of distance called a light-year – the distance light travels in one year at a speed of about 186,000 miles a second. A light-year is approximately six trillion miles (6,000,000,000,000). In these units, our nearest star is four light-years away, a typical galaxy is 100,000 light-years wide, and the average distance between galaxies is roughly three million light-years. Our nearest galactic neighbour is the Andromeda Galaxy, two million light-years from our own. No one knows exactly how large the universe is, but some of the most distant galaxies so far observed are well over ten billion light-years away. This is a distance so great that the light that now reaches us started its journey before the earth was even formed.

The Evidence for Astrology

Today's understanding of the enormity and complexity of the universe is worlds apart from the conceptions of the ancients. The Greeks, Romans and other archaic civilizations who founded the principles of astrology viewed the universe very differently. To them, the firmament of stars was only just out of reach, while the sun, moon and planets were the gods overseeing human destiny. From the scientific standpoint, the stars and planets are simply too far away to have any direct effect upon the daily life of planet earth. Astrologers may argue that there are other forces at work which science has not yet recognized. However, few scientists are prepared to speculate about something for which, in their opinion, there is no evidence.

In recent years the case for astrology (at least certain aspects of it) has been considerably strengthened. There may be, after all, measurable cosmic forces influencing human characteristics, personality and behaviour.

Although the stars may be too distant to affect our daily existence, the same is not true of the sun and moon. Apart from providing us with the heat and light necessary for survival, the sun (or at least the earth's angle to it) determines the seasons. The moon, on the other hand, exerts direct gravitational influence over the ocean tides. Moreover, the moon has long been associated with the human condition: its cycle closely corresponds to the female cycle, and its apparent effect on human behaviour resulted in the unfortunate word 'lunatic' being coined for people with a mental illness. Many renowned scientists have now discovered previously unsuspected solar and lunar influences on the human body.

Japan's Maki Takata has examined the influence of sunspot activity on blood pressure, discovering a close relationship between the two. Italy's Georgio Piccardi has shown that both sunspots and the cycle of the moon affect various chemical reactions in the body. And America's David Levinson has demonstrated that both men and women have a delicate sensitivity to the moon's gravitational field. But perhaps most astonishing, regarding astrology, is the work of the British research team led by Dr Lewis Atkinson in 1985.

Atkinson's research indicates that the moon's gravity directly influences the development of tiny organisms. Although the effect in fully-grown and complex life forms, such as humans, is minimal, it may well be sufficient to influence the embryo.

Although personality is shaped by environment, genetics moulds our basic character – our inbuilt starting point. That is why two young children may respond very differently to the same conditions; one clinging to an overbearing parent, another rebelling. Genetically inherited, these characteristics may be modified in the early development of the foetus by the gravitational influence of the moon.

To understand how the moon might affect genetic attributes, we must first appreciate that a living organism is actually a complex arrangement of self-replicating molecules. Simply described, the atoms that make up matter are comprised of a nucleus around which electrons move. When atoms exist in groups, bonded together, they are called molecules, and a substance comprised of only one type of atom is called an element. When atoms of different elements combine they form the molecules of a compound, with the properties often remarkably different from the original elements from which they were composed. For example, an atom of the soft metal sodium, which reacts explosively with water, and an atom of the poisonous gas chlorine, combine to form a molecule of edible common salt. The properties and behaviour of a substance often depends more on the shape of its molecules than on the atoms from which it is formed. It is in the tiny microcosm that the lunar effects on organisms occur.

A molecule known as deoxyribonucleic acid is responsible for life as we know it. Deoxyribonucleic acid, or DNA for short, is an incredible molecule, having the unique ability to reproduce itself. It is the essence of life itself, for without DNA the very cells which form a living organism could not divide and grow.

The DNA is concentrated in the nucleus of each cell, containing instructions as to what the cell should become. Some cells develop more efficient ways of breaking down food and become stomach cells, some acquire a hard membrane and make up skin, while others become sensitive to light and form eyes. Incredibly, the nucleus of a fertilized egg contains all the instructions for the development of a fully-grown creature. Called the genetic code, it determines everything from the colour of hair to the size of the nose.

The DNA at the heart of the cell can be thought of as a miniature computer programme, although infinitely more complex. We know that some external factors can damage or modify this program, such as chemical effects or radiation, which in extreme cases may result in deformity or mutation. Another influencing factor, demonstrated by the Atkinson research, is the gravitational pull of the moon.

The Atkinson findings suggest that the moon's gravity affects the internal cell structure by causing slight variations in the build up of nucleotides – the building blocks of DNA – during each 29½ day cycle of the moon. During a new moon, when the sun and moon are exerting a gravitational pull from the same direction, the influence is different from the time of a full moon, when the gravitational influence of the two bodies are from opposite directions. In a multi-cellular organism this has no noticeable influence, as the genetic program is already established. However, in the single cell of a fertilized egg the genetic coding can be subtly modified. Consequently, mental and physiological characteristics might well be modified by the moon at the time of conception or during foetal development.

There was also another interesting point in the Atkinson findings. The lunar effect varied depending on the time of year. Put simply, the lunar effect ran in roughly 28-day cycles which gradually altered as the year progressed. Although the moon cycles may influence our eventual characteristics, how might the changing seasons be involved?

Modern scientific studies have been made regarding the seasonal effects of sunlight upon the annual biological rhythms of organisms. The growth patterns of plants, such as blossom in spring, fruit in summer and leaf-fall in autumn, are completely synchronized with the seasons. Animals also experience seasonal alterations: hibernation in winter, breeding in spring, and migration in autumn, are just a few of the ways in which the animal kingdom responds to the seasons. These annual changes are due almost exclusively to the availability of sunlight; the organism responds to the lengthening and shortening of daylight. For example, following summer, around mid-September, when day and night are of equal duration, the tree is stimulated to start losing its leaves, while the squirrel prepares for hibernation. After winter, when day and night are again of equal duration around mid-March, the tree's leaves begin to grow and the squirrel awakes.

There can be little doubt that the length of daylight is the stimulus responsible for these changes. If a creature from the northern hemisphere is taken to the southern hemisphere, before long its behaviour patterns adapt;

the same is true for the growth of plants. The relocated animal does not hibernate in the height of summer, and tree's leaves do not fall in the spring.

Until recently humanity was considered immune to such seasonal rhythms. Modern studies, however, have discovered many variations in bodily and mental activity which correspond to seasonal change. In the wild, an alteration of behaviour and metabolism was essential for our ancestors' survival. The gathering and hoarding instinct was imperative during summer months for early humans to prepare for winter. Less activity was equally essential in winter when energy needed to be conserved. In most of us the seasonal response mechanisms are not overtly apparent. However, even in our technological world, where daily life continues to a large degree unaltered by summer or winter, a considerable number of people still respond to winter in an almost disabling manner.

In 1984 psychiatrists at the National Institute of Mental Health in Maryland, USA, were among the first to identify a syndrome known as the Seasonal Affected Disorder, or SAD for short. In autumn, shortly after the days become shorter than the nights, sufferers from SAD begin to feel their energy declining. They oversleep and have difficulty rising in the morning. However, even though they are sleeping more they still feel exceedingly tired during the day. Furthermore, they eat too much, especially carbohydrates, and their weight increases. Eventually they become lethargic, have difficulty thinking, processing information or carrying on with their work. Sometimes the problem can become so severe that they completely withdraw from social activities, and may even be unable to hold down a job. In extreme cases the syndrome is virtually incapacitating. Paradoxically, those with SAD are experiencing a condition which would have been immensely beneficial to their remote ancestors.

For years, psychiatrists and physicians failed to recognize the seasonal pattern of SAD, and traditional therapy and drug treatment had little or no benefit. It is now known that, like other creatures, SAD sufferers respond to the availability of daylight. Today, the condition is treated by tricking the patient's physiology into believing that it is summer all year round. Standard artificial lighting is not sufficiently bright to simulate daylight, but by exposing the patient to high-luminosity fluorescent lights for two hours every morning, SAD is alleviated in nearly all sufferers. Exposure to light the intensity of sunlight just after dawn, light therapy, as it is called, makes the patient's sunlight responsive system believe that the days are longer than they actually are. With light therapy the patient quickly returns to summertime alertness.

These seasonal responses to sunlight and other yearly changes are known as circannual rhythms, and are responsible for many other subtle variations in bodily activity, including hormonal balance. Although detailed study is still in its early stages, it is known that a human foetus is modified by the circannual rhythms of its mother. Infants who undergo specific stages of embryonic development at the same time of year may therefore share characteristic behavioural and physiological traits. In other words, someone conceived in December, for example, will be affected differently to someone conceived in June. The eventual date of birth may therefore be an important factor in determining various aspects of the child's psychology and physiology. As pregnancy is nine months duration for almost every human being, most of us will have undergone foetal development during the same seasons as another who shares our birthday.

Circannual physiological alteration and behavioural change may account for the apparent accuracy of astrology. The date of birth may help determine human characteristics and also be responsible for certain aspects of behaviour at different times of the year. Someone born in Aries, for instance, would have undergone foetal development during the same seasonal period as another born in the same sign, and consequently would have experienced similar embryonic modifications. Someone born in Taurus, on the other hand, would have experienced slightly different modifications, shared by other Taureans. Not only might they be similar in personality, they are also likely to behave in a similar manner at the same times of year. This may explain how astrology could predict that during the sign of Capricorn, in the middle of winter, a Virgo may do one thing and a Gemini another.

In modern astrology the exact time and place of birth is needed to compile what many believe to be an accurate horoscope. The precise positions of the sun, moon and planets are then plotted and their relative positions in the zodiac are interpreted. The popular horoscope, however, concerns solely the sun's position in the zodiac, and so, it is argued, is only broadly applicable. Consequently, the apparent accuracy of modern sun-sign astrology in predicting general human characteristics and behaviour may well be the result of circannual rhythms.

These latest scientific discoveries are of particular relevance to the present book. *Novacosm – The Original Zodiac* reveals a lunar zodiac used by ancient Babylonians centuries before the modern zodiac was devised. Unlike the modern zodiac, its horoscopes did not incorporate the positions of the stars and planets, but the cycles of the moon and the seasons of the year. An individual was thought to be influenced by both the time of year and the lunar month in which they were born. Accordingly, they incorporated the seasonal *and* the lunar influences – both of which are now being shown to subtly influence human characteristics. It therefore seems quite within the realms of scientific feasibility that this lunar zodiac – devised nearly 3000 years ago – might really be a means of predicting human behaviour.

Graham Phillips
London 1994

PREFACE
What is the Novacosm?

VIRGO, Cancer and the other constellations familiar to us today were not the original zodiac signs. The modern twelve-sign zodiac was invented by the Greeks around 450 BC, but an older thirteen-sign zodiac was devised by the Babylonians at least three centuries earlier. This early zodiac is known from 2500-year-old texts discovered during excavations at Nimrud, the capital of ancient Assyria, in 1960, although its importance to astrology has been completely overlooked. Not only was this early zodiac based around the cycles of the moon rather than sun signs, it also employed images very different from those familiar today. Instead of Aries, Taurus, Gemini and so forth, its signs included some very exotic creatures, such as a griffin, a phoenix, and a sphinx. So now for the first time after nearly 3000 years, this original zodiac can be used to cast horoscopes.

Unfortunately, there is no surviving record of what this lunar zodiac was originally called, and a name is needed for convenience sake. As the system is new to the modern world and concerns the skies, I have coined the word 'Novacosm', from the Latin word *nova*, meaning new, and the Greek word *cosmos*, meaning the heavens.

In the first introductory section, 'Astrology and the

Original Zodiac', the discovery and reconstruction of this ancient zodiac is described. The second introductory section, 'The Novacosm', includes and explains a simple chart from which to discover your own Novacosm sign. The remainder of the book focuses on each of the Novacosm signs, with a character analysis and relevant predictions for each.

Novacosm: The Original Zodiac is not intended to challenge the traditional horoscope; rather it presents an alternative and equally enlightening astrological system.

Melissa Marshall
London 1994

ASTROLOGY AND
THE ORIGINAL ZODIAC

The History of Astrology

THE earliest celestial observations survive in the
form of stone tablets from Mesopotamia, in what
is now Iraq. Over four thousand years old, they show
that eclipses of the sun and moon were seen as omens of
conflict and natural disaster. Consequently, they are
not simply a record of astronomy, the observations of
the heavens, but astrology, the interpretation of the
heavens.

As time passed, ancient civilizations throughout the
world began to document the motions of the sun and
moon, and their relative positions when significant
events occurred. It was in ancient Babylon, about three
thousand years ago, that modern astrology began, with
the invention of the zodiac.

To chart the course of the year, a circle was imagined
in the heavens; the path that the sun appeared to follow
in its annual cycle. Represented as a wheel, it was
divided into equal segments, one for each month. Each
section, called a sign, was named after a constellation of
stars that lay within it. In other words, to say that the
sun was in a particular sign meant that it had entered the
area of sky dominated by that constellation. This
wheel, or imaginary band of sky, was later called the
zodiac, from the Greek word *zodiakos* meaning 'of

animals'; so named because most of its constellations bore the name of a living creature, such as the bull, the ram and the crab.

How did the constellations get their names? Clearly, they are not recognizable in the pictorial sense. Who could claim, for example, that the stars that make up Taurus look anything like a bull, or that Aries remotely resembles a ram?

The early astrologers believed that the birth date was responsible for human characteristics, and the zodiac sign in which the sun was present at that time was deemed responsible. The sign was then named after a creature or mythical being which best symbolized the character traits of those born in the sign, and the constellation was eventually incorporated into this pictorial image. Consequently, the person born with the sun in the sign of Aries, for instance, had not inherited ram-like qualities because the constellation looked like a ram, but the ram was chosen for the sign once ram-like qualities had been observed in people born at that time.

This modern zodiac was invented by the Greeks in the fifth century BC. The earlier Babylonians used a different system: a thirteen-sign lunar zodiac. The cycles of the moon, or lunar months, were considered the chief influence upon human characteristics, not the zodiac sun signs employed today.

The term 'month' was originally derived from the word moon, and referred to the period of a lunar cycle, from new moon to new moon. The Babylonian calendar was derived from the approximately 29-day lunar months, beginning each year on the new moon immediately preceding the spring equinox around 21 March. (A lunar month is more precisely 29.53 days in length.) Because there are about twelve and a third lunar cycles in a year, some years had twelve months and others had thirteen. The later Greeks and Romans abandoned the lunar cycles as the basis for their calendar, and standardized the year into twelve roughly equal months that no longer bore any relationship to the cycles of the moon. Accordingly, it was easy for them to devise a twelve-sign zodiac which corresponded precisely with their divisions of the solar year. The moon's position in the zodiac at the time of birth was taken into consideration in Greek astrology, but this 'moon sign', as it is now called, was very different to the Babylonian lunar cycle.

Ultimately, the Romans altered the calendar and renamed the months after their own gods and emperors (for example, July after Julius Caesar, August after the emperor Augustus, and March after the god Mars). These new months were roughly thirty days in length and no longer aligned with the zodiac constellations. This is why the zodiac signs now begin around the 21st of each modern month and not at the beginning.

Once the zodiac was created, and the significance of each sign established, astrologers were free to take the final step in the development of astrology – the casting of the horoscope. Derived from the Greek words *hora*, time, and *skopos*, to observe, the word horoscope means literally an observation of a moment in time. This is exactly what a horoscope is; a chart diagramatically depicting the heavens at the time of birth. The earliest surviving Greek horoscope dates from the fourth century BC, and shows that by interpreting the positions of the sun, moon and planets in the zodiac, the astrologer would predict a child's eventual personality, and foretell the likely path of their life. (Because they are all on approximately the same orbital plane around the sun, the planets only move through the zodiac and no other constellations. The moon also only moves through the zodiac, as its earth orbit is on a roughly equivalent plane.)

Although the Greeks invented the modern horoscope, it was the Romans who established Western astrology throughout the world. From Britain to India, from Africa to the Steppes of Russia, the zodiac came into popular use. Through the fall of the Roman Empire, the tumultuous Dark Ages and the turbulent medieval era, astrology survived. However, although the sun, moon and planets are all of significance in the horoscope, it is the sun that has assumed greatest importance in modern astrology.

The stellar constellation, or zodiac sign, covered by the sun at the moment of birth is often referred to as the 'star sign'. A more accurate term, however, is the 'sun sign'. There can be few people in the West who do not know their sun sign; every day, newspapers and magazines throughout the world carry horoscopes and astrological columns, each predicting what the stars have in store for the eager reader. For your personal prediction, all you need know is your sun sign. Whether Virgo, Capricorn or Libra, across the globe your future is revealed in print.

There are basically two types of astrology; natal and forecast. Natal astrology is the interpretation of the horoscope regarding character and personality, while forecast astrology is the prediction of events based on the movements of the heavenly bodies. Each individual sun sign is thought to be influenced by the positions of the moon and planets and their place in the zodiac. The moon in Cancer, for example, is seen to affect a Virgoan differently to a Sagittarian. Although natal astrology is universally popular, it is forecast astrology that has secured a prime place in the world's media.

Interestingly, it was only in 1930 that sun signs found their way into the popular press. It began in London, when the editor of the *Sunday Express* invited the celebrated astrologer R. H. Naylor to cast the horoscope of the newly-born Princess Margaret. Although it was only intended to be a one-off contribution, the popular response was such that he was asked to make further predictions the following week.

Whether by fate, luck or skill, one of Naylor's predictions was to prove so uncannily accurate that the world sat up and took notice. In his column Naylor suggested that a British aircraft might be in danger, and on the day of publication the airship R-101 crashed in Northern France. The newspaper gave Naylor massive publicity and persuaded him to write a regular column. Naylor decided to divide his column into twelve paragraphs, one for each sun sign. All his readers need to was to consult their sign and find the relevant prediction.

The column became so popular that newspapers around the world began employing their own astrologers to run regular columns in Naylor's style – and so the newspaper horoscope was born.

Whether it be sun-sign, moon-sign or planetary astrology, or if it is natal or forecast astrology, all modern horoscopes in the western tradition use the zodiac originally devised by the ancient Greeks in the fifth century BC. There was, however, a very different zodiac, devised in ancient Babylon many centuries earlier.

The Babylonian Zodiac

Founded around 2000 BC, Babylon was one of the greatest cities of the ancient world. It was capital of the Mesopotamian kingdom of Babylonia in modern Iraq.

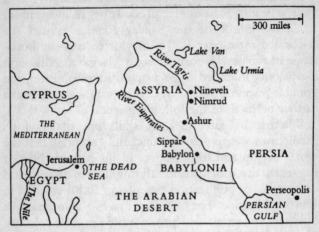

Ancient Mesopotamia and the Eastern Mediterranean

During the seventh century BC Babylonia was progressively annexed by the Assyrians, although it again rose to prominence after 612 BC when the Assyrian Empire collapsed. Free of Assyrian domination, Babylon became the cultural capital of the world. The ruins of Babylon which still survive are the remains of the citadel built by the famous king Nebuchadnezzar in the early sixth century BC.

According to the Greek historian Herodotus, the city was a massive stronghold surrounded by fortifications some 14 miles square. Three hundred feet high and 85 feet thick, the perimeter walls were so huge that horsedrawn chariots were needed to patrol the battlements. The River Euphrates divided the city and further walls protected the banks, interspersed with gates of burnished bronze. Through the centre of Babylon ran a broad processional way which led out of the city via the Ishtar Gate, an impregnable entrance crowned with gigantic towers and carvings of enormous animals.

At the administrative heart of the city stood the royal palace, built around an enormous temple sacred to the chief god Marduk. The entire complex was surrounded by one of the seven wonders of the ancient world: the Hanging Gardens of Babylon, brick terraces covered with exotic trees and plants brought from every corner of the empire. The gardens were so spectacular that even wild animals were left to roam free amongst the foliage.

Although Babylonian astrological observations survive from around 1000 BC, much of what is known of Babylonian astrology comes from discoveries made during archaeological excavations of the Assyrian capital Nimrud. Between 1957 and 1963 the dig unearthed the remains of Fort Shalmaneser, a huge palace-fortress built by the Assyrians around 840 BC. Amongst the treasures discovered were artefacts accumulated from all over the Middle East, including Babylonian astrological tablets dating from the period of the Assyrian occupation. Unfortunately, no precise description of Babylonian astrology has been discovered, but from various scripts and carvings a broad picture has emerged.

The Babylonian calendar was divided into thirteen lunar cycles, each having a specific religious significance. Because the number of lunar cycles does not divide exactly into a solar year (twelve lunar months is approximately 354 days, which is 11.25 days short of the solar year) the Babylonian calendar varied. Most years had twelve months, but in order to continually realign the lunar months with the solar year, every few years an extra month was included. Known as the intercalary month, it was similar to the modern practice of adding an extra day every leap year.

*The Babylonian lunar zodiac. From the King Sargon astrological
text (circa 710 BC) found during the Nimrud excavations.
Now in the Aleppo Museum, Syria.*

The Babylonian New Year started at the beginning
of the growing season and the first month, known as
Nisan, always included the most important religious
festival, the spring equinox, around 21 March. Every
month began on the new moon and so New Year's Day
would always be the day of the new moon immediately
preceding the spring equinox. It could therefore fall
anywhere between late February and mid-March. If a
particular year began early there would be thirteen
complete lunar cycles before the following *Nisan* and so
the intercalary month was needed. This occurred about
once every three years.

In modern astrology the zodiac constellation in
which the sun is present at the time of birth is considered a chief influence upon fate and personality. The
Babylonians, however, considered the lunar month of

birth to be the determining factor. In ancient Babylon during the New Year festival, *Akitu*, the high priest, the *sheshgallu*, would travel the processional way predicting the destinies of important citizens for the coming year. The destiny of each individual would depend on the lunar cycle in which they had been born. For example, someone born in the third lunar cycle of a particular year would be thought to fare differently to someone born in the fifth cycle. It therefore seems that the thirteen-sign zodiac was a list of lunar 'birth signs'.

All we know of this lunar zodiac survives on ivory writing-boards dating from the eighth century BC. One such text discovered at Nimrud, is believed to have been prepared for the Assyrian King Sargon around 710 BC. It includes the following images to represent the lunar months:

Lunar Cycle	Symbol
1	A vase and a fish
2	A firebird
3	A hero
4	A winged ibex (a goat)
5	A genie
6	A griffin
7	An oryx (an antelope)
8	A man riding an eagle
9	A serpent
10	A dragon
11	A sphinx
12	A swallow
13	A huntress

This lunar zodiac does not appear to have been a list of stellar constellations. The zodiac is the band of sky through which the sun, moon and planets appear to move as seen from earth, and not, as is often thought, the name for the constellations themselves. Accordingly, this Babylonian lunar zodiac may not necessarily have related to the stars. Unlike the sun, due to the nature of its orbit around the earth, the moon appears to move 'randomly' through the constellations. On the same day each year the sun will always be in the same constellation, whereas the moon can appear in various zodiac signs. It is therefore difficult to imagine how the stellar zodiac could have been divided into constellations which corresponded only with the movements of the moon. It seems far more likely that the signs related to the lunar months, and was therefore a lunar zodiac.

The thirteen images probably represented the god, spirit, or mythical being with which each month was associated. Unfortunately, not all are known with certainty: the first month seems to have been sacred to Nanshe, the water goddess, as it was represented by the glyph depicting a vase and a fish. The heroic figure of the third month was probably the mythical hero Gilgamesh. The winged ibex of the fourth month was seemingly a legendary creature called Assari. And the huntress of the intercalary, thirteenth month was probably Ishtar, a principal Babylonian deity.

The lunar cycles themselves are easy enough to reconstruct: simply consult a published astronomical chart (an ephemeris) containing the lunar cycles for any given year. Each new moon immediately preceding the spring equinox is where the Babylonian year begins. If thirteen full cycles occur before the following spring equinox a thirteenth month is included. The pressing question for astrology, however, is how the Babylonians considered someone born in any particular lunar cycle to be influenced.

The first month, for example, was seemingly governed by the water goddess; her influence would presumably have been seen in an individual's life and personality. A person born in that month was probably thought to have been endowed with the characteristics of fast-flowing water – quick, changeable and energetic. Someone born in the third cycle, represented by the hero, may similarly have been thought a brave and successful warrior. But because little is known of the mythology associated with many of the signs, we must look further afield if we are to reconstruct the entire system.

Fortunately, much of Babylonian mythology was preserved in other, later cultures. Babylon had been a cultural crossroads for centuries and many ancient civilizations adopted their mythology from Babylon. The Babylonian creation myth, for instance, occurs in both Assyrian and Persian mythology. It was the Greeks, however, who were most influenced by Babylonian culture after they occupied the city in 330 BC. The mythology concerning many of the Babylonian zodiac signs may consequently be preserved in the Greek equivalent.

The sign of the first month was a vase and a fish, and the water goddess Nanshe was represented by a vase in which a fish swam. She was the daughter of Ea, the water god, venerated during the first month of *Nisan*. Little is known of the mythology concerning her, except that a special ceremony took place in her honour each year to ensure a plentiful rainfall. On the Euphrates a flotilla of boats escorted a sacred barge containing a statue or a priestess representing the goddess. By the time of the Assyrian occupation Ea had completely taken over her role as water deity in Babylonian religion. Consequently, when the surviving lunar zodiac was compiled, around 700 BC, she was simply the spirit of the waterfall. Now called Cascaya, her symbol was still the vase and fish, and in statues of the period she is often holding such items.

The sign for the second month was a firebird. Little is known of the Babylonian firebird, although it may have been the same mythical creature described by the Greeks as the Phoenix. Around 450 BC the Greek historian Herodotus mentions for the first time this exotic bird, believed to be reborn in the Arabian Desert every five hundred years. It was said to resemble an eagle which flew from the desert to the temple of Heliopolis in Egypt. After five centuries it would burn to dust, ultimately to rise again from its own ashes. Those who told Herodotus of the legend were his Egyptian guides, and accordingly it has been suggested that the Phoenix was an Egyptian myth, originating with the Egyptian bird-god Bennu. However, the reincarnating firebird is unknown in older Egyptian mythology; moreover, Bennu was usually represented as a heron, not an eagle. As the only earlier depictions of a firebird survive in the Babylonian zodiac, it is far more likely that the Phoenix was originally one of its signs.

The hero of the third month is probably the epic quest hero Gilgamesh. He was undoubtedly the most important of the Babylonian heroes, as many versions of his story survive. The Epic of Gilgamesh was first discovered in the nineteenth century at the ruins of the temple of Nabu in Nineveh. Further tablets of this twelve-chapter epic were found at Sippar (modern Abu Habba) in the early 1900s, and just before the outbreak of the First World War German excavations at Ashur discovered an Assyrian version of the same text.

Gilgamesh was a youthful prince who embarked upon a search for immortality. Although he failed in his ultimate quest, on his journey he was forced to slay malevolent creatures, such as the giant forest-ogre

Humbaba and Anu, the terrible Bull of Heaven. In the lunar zodiac the hero is depicted as standing on the head of an ogre, almost certainly Humbaba whom Gilgamesh decapitated. The Greeks interpolated Gilgamesh into their own mythology as Hercules. Like his forbear Gilgamesh, Hercules undertakes an epic quest during which he destroys many strange beasts, such as the nine-headed Hydra and the savage Nemean lion.

Assari, the winged ibex (a type of goat) of the fourth month is known from statues found at Nimrud. Assari became a flying horse in Assyrian mythology, which in turn became Pegasus, the winged horse of Greek legend.

The figure representing the fifth month holds a pine cone, used in ancient times to sprinkle scented water during ceremonial rituals. He is almost certainly a genie, as they were usually depicted holding such pine cones. Although the genie became a principal figure in later Arabian legend, the original genii were Babylonian spirits of protection. They were benevolent beings who acted as personal guardians and as messengers from the gods.

The griffin of the sixth month may originally have been Tammuz, one of two doorkeepers who guarded the chamber of the great gods. Dating from the first millenium BC, his image has been found in gigantic statues at entrances to ruined temples throughout Mesopotamia. The Tammuz statues depict a being with the head of a man, the body of a lion and the wings of an eagle. The sixth month is represented by such a figure although it is an eagle's head instead of a man's.

The griffin was absorbed into both Assyrian and Greek mythology as a mythical beast set to guard hidden treasure. Not only is the griffin's role as guardian similar to Tammuz, but it too was depicted as part lion and part eagle, although the human element was dropped. The griffin can still be found in modern heraldry, where it has the body, tail and hind legs of a lion, and the head, forelegs and wings of an eagle.

The seventh month was represented by an oryx, the sacred antelope of both the Babylonians and the Assyrians. The rare creature was believed to have magical properties and represent creativity and imagination.

The eagle-riding man of the eighth month was almost certainly Etana. In the Babylonian Epic of Etana, he is a legendary king who, in order to secure an heir, searches for a magical plant of fertility. Eventually his quest leads him to Heaven itself, to which he flies on the back of a giant eagle.

There are a number of serpents and dragons in Babylonian mythology, and so the specific creatures associated with the ninth and tenth months remain unidentified. Serpents and dragons appear in mythology from all over the Middle East, where the dragon is usually a feared and powerful fire-breathing beast and the serpent is a symbol of knowledge and wisdom. The lunar zodiac images of the serpent and the dragon would have stood for similar themes.

The sphinx of the eleventh month is female, unlike the Egyptian sphinx which was usually male. The sphinx, a lion with a human head, figured in Egyptian, Assyrian and Babylonian art, although it is uncertain in which country it originated. Surprisingly little is known about sphinx mythology until the Greeks portrayed it as a female entity who destroyed travellers who failed to answer a riddle. The sphinx eventually killed herself when the hero Oedipus answered correctly.

Nothing has survived concerning the twelfth-month swallow image in either Babylonian or Assyrian texts.

Some depict a swan for this month, but again nothing is known regarding its place in Babylonian legend. The swan eventually played an important role in Greek mythology as Cygnus, son of the sun god Apollo. When he was abandoned by his closest companion Phylius, Cygnus threw himself into the waters of Lake Canopus where he was turned into a swan by his father.

As the thirteenth intercalary month only occurred every few years it was a particularly sacred time. The Babylonian lunar zodiac shows a female figure with a bow for this month. She seems to be a huntress or female warrior, which links her with the most important Babylonian female deity, Ishtar. Like the month, Ishtar was special. She was not only the goddess of love, but also of battle. As a love goddess she had a place in the heavens as the planet Venus, and as a female warrior the great entrance to Babylon was sacred to her. Indeed, she was the guardian of the city. In Greek mythology she became Athena, both a warrior and a peace goddess and the protector of Athens, after whom the city was named and the Parthenon dedicated.

From an analysis of these related legends, a list of some of the Babylonian lunar zodiac spirits and their classical counterparts emerged, as shown in the table on page 16.

The Re-Creation of the Lunar Zodiac

The $64,000 question – could this 3000-year-old zodiac still be used today? To put it to the test, I decided to conduct an experiment. I compiled a list of friends and associates – about a dozen born in each cycle – and asked them to complete a questionnaire: likes, dislikes, hobbies, pastimes, employment, health and so forth. Astonishingly, those born in the same cycle appeared to share similar characteristics. Those born in the first

Lunar Cycle	Symbol	Babylonian	Classical
1	A vase and a fish	Cascaya or Nanshe	
2	A firebird		Phoenix
3	A hero	Gilgamesh	Hercules
4	A winged ibex	Assari	Pegasus
5	A genie		
6	A griffin	Tammuz	
7	An oryx		
8	A man riding an eagle	Etana	
9	A serpent		
10	A dragon		
11	A sphinx		
12	A swallow		Cygnus
13	A huntress	Ishtar	Athena

Babylonian and classical lunar zodiac spirits.

cycle seemed to be romantics, whereas those with marked financial acumen were generally born in the third cycle. Musicians were mostly born in the sixth cycle, academics in the seventh, and artists and skilled craftspeople in the fourth. The tenth cycle included those with an abundance of nervous energy, while the twelfth included those who seemed to be far more serene. The most expressive were born in the ninth, the most impulsive in the eighth, and the most imaginative in the thirteenth.

Although a far wider and more detailed study was necessary, something immediately struck me about the results. The apparent characteristics of the cycle seemed to correlate with the month image. For example, those born in the third month seemed to possess marked leadership qualities, and the image for the month was a hero. Those born in the second cycle seemed to have the enviable ability to fight back when circumstances became difficult, and the Phoenix, which rose from its own ashes, has long been a symbol of overcoming hardship. Although the findings were limited, it seemed that, like the solar zodiac, a symbol best typifying the predominant traits of those born in each sign may have been chosen to represent them.

A more detailed and expert survey was needed. I asked a psychologist to help me prepare an extended questionnaire and over the course of a year completed about a hundred for each cycle. Repeatedly, the results were similar, which I now include in the following chapters.

In order to recreate the original lunar zodiac as authentically as possible, I have employed the traditional style of natal astrology – a birth sign analysis for each cycle, linking it with the mythology associated with each lunar month.

The ancient Babylonians not only derived character readings from the lunar zodiac, they also used it to make predictions. Numerous clay tablets dating from the middle of the first millennium BC show that natural phenomena, such as floods or sand storms, occurring in certain months were considered omens or portents for the kingdom's future. The individual months were also thought to hold a separate fate or fortune in store for those born in different lunar signs. For example, a person born in the month of the griffin was expected to fare differently in the month of the serpent than, say, someone born in the month of the sphinx or the dragon. Unlike classical astrology, where the supposed influences of the planets in the zodiac signs are known, only an outline of Babylonian lunar forecast astrology has survived.

In essence, it seems that the influences of the birth sign and the current lunar cycle were thought to combine. For example, as the dragon ruled over mental activity, in the dragon month a high level of mental activity would be expected in many individuals. Some signs would benefit during the dragon month: the hero-born would be stronger, the serpent-born more erudite and the sphinx-born more cunning. Other signs would suffer: the oryx-born would overwork, the swallow-born would be restless and the huntress-born would make reckless decisions. The same lunar influence was therefore thought to affect those born in different signs in different ways. (Of course, those that suffered in one month would benefit in another, and vice versa.)

Accordingly, the circumstances likely to occur in a person's life were considered predictable. Again using the example of the dragon month: as someone born in the serpent sign was expected to be particularly erudite, during the dragon cycle they would especially benefit from their powers of persuasion. Consequently, it could be foretold that during the month of the dragon, a serpent-born would make new friends and allies. Alternatively, someone born in the huntress sign would be predicted to suffer disappointments due to a foolhardy attitude.

Some of the predictions made by the Babylonian astrologers initially seem less methodical. On what logical grounds, for instance, did they foretell that someone born in the sphinx month could expect the arrival of surprise news in the month of the serpent? A possible explanation might be that they were likely to share similar types of friends, which consequently would be born in the same sign. Those born in the serpent sign, for example, might have been thought impelled to contact their sphinx-born acquaintances by lunar influences affecting them in the same way at the same time.

I decided to discover if people born in the same cycle today really did share common experiences during the same lunar months. I asked a number of my volunteers from each sign to consult their diaries for the last few years and note the most significant events that occurred in each lunar month. In general, it seemed that similar circumstances did indeed surround those who shared the same sign, during the same lunar cycles.

From these, and subsequent observations, I have included a brief 'Fate and Fortune' section at the end of each sign chapter. Similar to the character readings, the predictions are coupled with the symbolism of the lunar zodiac.

THE NOVACOSM

THE lunar zodiac outlined in the following chapters incorporates the moon cycles used by the Babylonians, and character similes reconstructed from mythology and presented from a modern perspective.

The Novacosm has thirteen signs, corresponding with the thirteen moon cycles of the lunar zodiac. Each sign is named after the mythical beings with which the cycle appears associated:

First Cycle	– Cascaya
Second Cycle	– the Phoenix
Third Cycle	– the Hero
Fourth Cycle	– Assari
Fifth Cycle	– the Genie
Sixth Cycle	– the Griffin
Seventh Cycle	– the Oryx
Eighth Cycle	– Etana
Ninth Cycle	– the Serpent
Tenth Cycle	– the Dragon
Eleventh Cycle	– the Sphinx
Twelfth Cycle	– the Swallow
Thirteenth Cycle	– the Huntress

Anyone born in the first cycle is born in the sign of Cascaya, the second cycle, the Phoenix, and so on. As there are twelve complete cycles of the moon every year, the first twelve signs repeat annually, whereas the thirteenth sign, the Huntress, only occurs on average every three years.

The Novacosm commences with the day of the new moon immediately preceding the spring equinox (or in the southern hemisphere, the autumn equinox). Due to the arrangement of our modern calendar, the spring equinox (when day and night are of equal length) varies from one year to the next, usually between 20 and 22 March. On average it falls on 21 March and so this date is used for convenience. The Babylonian day actually ran from sundown to sundown, although to bring the Novacosm in line with today's calendar its days start at midnight in the normal way. The first cycle therefore begins on, and includes, the days of the new moon immediately before 21 March.

The following chart shows the dates of the new moons for 1962, 1963 and 1964:

Year	1962	1963	1964
Jan	6	25	14
Feb	5	24	13
Mar	6	24	14
Apr	4	23	12
May	4	23	11
Jun	2	21	10
Jul	2,31	20	9
Aug	30	19	7
Sep	28	17	6
Oct	28	17	5
Nov	27	16	4
Dec	26	16	4

In 1962 the new moon immediately preceding 21 March was on 6 March, and so the Novacosm year began on that day. The first cycle ran until the next new moon on 4 April. As the day of the new moon is the first day of any cycle, the first cycle actually ended at midnight on 3 April. In that year anyone born on, or between, 6 March and 3 April was born in the first sign, Cascaya. The second cycle began on 4 April and continued until the day before the next new moon on 4 May. In that year anyone born on, or between, 4 April and 3 May was born in the second sign, the Phoenix. The cycles continued until the following year when the twelfth lunar cycle ended with the new moon preceding 21 March.

In 1963 the Novacosm commenced once more with Cascaya on 24 February. However, in that year the Novacosm began early, in February rather than March. There were therefore twelve complete lunar cycles before the new moon on 13 February the following year – two new moons before 21 March. Consequently, in 1964 the thirteenth sign, the Huntress, was included.

This example demonstrates that the dates of each sign vary from year to year. On pages 24–27, therefore, there is a simple chart showing the individual signs for each year, from 1900 to 2000. The chapters that follow then focus on the different Novacosm signs, providing a character reading for each.

How to Use the Sign Chart

The vertical column on the far left indicates the year of birth:

        1960:
        1961:
        1962:

If you were born in 1960, for example, consult line 1960:

Year	Jan	Feb	Mar	Apr	May	Jun	Jul	Aug	Sep	Oct	Nov	Dec
1960	K 28	L 26	A 27	B 25	C 25	D 24	E 23	F 22	G 20	H 20	I 18	J 18

The horizontal rows show the lunar cycles for each year. The dates of the new moons are indicated by the numbers, and the Novacosm signs are represented by the letters:

A – Cascaya
B – the Phoenix
C – the Hero
D – Assari
E – the Genie
F – the Griffin
G – the Oryx
H – Etana
I – the Serpent
J – the Dragon
K – the Sphinx
L – the Swallow
M – the Huntress

Your Novacosm sign is determined by your date of birth. To discover your Novacosm sign, follow down the vertical column showing your birthday month until you reach the horizontal row showing your year of birth. As a new moon, this date is the beginning of a lunar cycle. Consequently, if your birthday falls on, or later than that date, your Novacosm sign is represented by the letter to the immediate right. Conversely, if your birthday is earlier than that date, then your Novacosm sign is represented by the letter to the immediate left.

An example of how this works follows the sign chart on the next four pages:

SIGN CHART

Year		Jan		Feb		Mar		Apr		May	
1900:		IK31	L			1A30	B	29	C	28	D
1901:	K	20	L	19	M	20	A	18	B	18	C
1902:	J	9	K	8	L	10	A	8	B	7	C
1903:	K	28	L	27	A	29	B	27	C	26	D
1904:	K	17	L	16	M	17	A	15	B	15	C
1905:	J	5	K	4	L	6	A	4	B	4	C
1906:	K	24	L	23	A	24	B	23	C	23	D
1907:	K	14	L	12	M	14	A	12	B	12	C
1908:	J	3	K	2	L	2	A	1B30	C	30	D
1909:	K	22	L	20	M	21	A	20	B	19	C
1910:	J	11	K	10	L	11	A	9	B	9	C
1911:	K	30	L			1A30	B	28	C	28	D
1912:	K	19	L	18	M	18	A	17	B	16	C
1913:	J	7	K	6	L	8	A	6	B	6	C
1914:	K	26	L	25	A	26	B	25	C	25	D
1915:	K	15	L	14	M	15	A	14	B	14	C
1916:	J	5	K	3	L	4	A	2	B	2C31	D
1917:	K	23	L	21	A	23	B	21	C	21	D
1918:	K	12	L	11	M	12	A	11	B	10	C
1919:	J	2	K	31	L	2A31	B	30	C	29	D
1920:	K	21	L	19	M	20	A	18	B	18	C
1921:	J	9	K	8	L	9	A	8	B	7	C
1922:	K	27	L	26	A	28	B	27	C	26	D
1923:	K	17	L	15	M	17	A	16	B	15	C
1924:	J	6	K	5	L	5	A	4	B	3	C
1925:	K	24	L	23	A	24	B	23	C	22	D
1926:	K	14	L	12	M	14	A	12	B	11	C
1927:	J	3	K	2	L	3	A	2	B	1C30	D
1928:	K	22	L	21	M	21	A	20	B	19	C
1929:	J	11	K	9	L	11	A	9	B	9	C
1930:	K	29	L	28	A	30	B	28	C	28	D
1931:	K	18	L	17	M	19	A	18	B	17	C
1932:	J	7	K	6	L	7	A	6	B	5	C
1933:	K	25	L	24	A	26	B	24	C	24	D
1934:	K	15	L	14	M	15	A	13	B	13	C
1935:	J	5	K	3	L	5	A	3	B	2	C
1936:	K	24	L	22	A	23	B	21	C	20	D
1937:	K	12	L	11	M	12	A	11	B	10	C
1938:	J	1K31	L			2 A31	B	30	C	29	D
1939:	K	20	L	19	M	21	A	19	B	19	C
1940:	J	9	K	8	L	9	A	7	B	7	C
1941:	K	27	L	26	A	27	B	26	C	26	D
1942:	K	16	L	15	M	16	A	15	B	15	C
1943:	J	6	K	4	L	6	A	4	B	4	C
1944:	K	25	L	24	A	24	B	22	C	22	D
1945:	K	14	L	12	M	14	A	12	B	11	C
1946:	J	3	K	2	L	3	A	2	B	1C30	D
1947:	K	22	L	21	A	22	B	21	C	20	D
1948:	K	11	L	10	M	10	A	9	B	9	C
1949:	K	29	L	27	A	29	B	28	C	27	D
1950:	K	18	L	16	M	18	A	17	B	17	C
1951:	J	7	K	6	L	7	A	6	B	6	C

3. The sign between December and January:

The cycle that falls between December and January of any year is indicated by the letter immediately before the January new moon date – the first letter in every horizontal row. In other words, if your birthday falls in December and is on or later than the date shown in the December column, the letter representing your Novacosm sign will be found at the beginning of the next line (i.e. before the January date of the following year). In 1961, for example, anyone born on or after December 8 would have their Novacosm sign represented by the letter J – the Dragon – the first sign of 1962:

Year	Jan	Feb	Mar	Apr	May	Jun	Jul	Aug	Sep	Oct	Nov	Dec
1961	K 16	L 15	M 16	A 15	B 14	C 13	D 12	E 11	F 10	G 9	H 8	I 8
1962	J 6	K 5	L 6	A 4	B 4	C 2	D 2	E31	F 30	G 28	H 28	I 27	J 26

Once you have discovered your Novacosm sign consult the relevant chapter that follows. Each Novacosm sign appears in order, with the chapter headed by the name of the lunar cycle and the code letter from the above chart.

Regarding the 'Fate and Fortune' section at the end of each chapter: to discover a particular or current lunar month, simply consult the moon chart in the usual way. Each lunar month runs between each of the dates in the horizontal row. It begins at and includes the date in each month column and continues until the day before the date in the subsequent row. The lunar cycle in question is represented by the letter between the two dates as shown above. For example, if you wanted to know the relevant dates for a Cascaya month, it would be indicated by the letter A, and be applicable to the days that fell between the dates to either side of the letter A.

One final note before consulting the following chapters. In reality the lunar influences which appear to determine the characteristics for each sign do not end and begin abruptly on the precise dates of the new moons. The changeover of influences from one cycle to the next is more gradual. Those born near the beginning or end of any cycle may find that they share characteristics in common with the nearest adjacent sign, and so it may also be worth consulting.

Finally, as it is necessary to consult the sign chart to accurately discover a particular lunar cycle, unless you have a remarkable memory, it is impossible to tell someone their sign without having the chart to hand. As a rough guide, therefore, here are the approximate modern months for each sign:

March	– Cascaya
April	– the Phoenix
May	– the Hero
June	– Assari
July	– the Genie
August	– the Griffin
September	– the Oryx
October	– Etana
November	– the Serpent
December	– the Dragon
January	– the Sphinx
February	– the Swallow

The majority of those born in each sign will have been born in these months. Even those who were not will usually have been born close enough to have been influenced to some degree by the sign indicated. However, it is only an approximation and does not include the intermittent thirteenth sign. The sign chart will obviously be needed for a more accurate reading.

CASCAYA

Approximate Calendar Month
MARCH

Sign Chart Letter
A

CASCAYA

In Babylonian mythology Cascaya was the spirit of the waterfall, an intangible figure, barely discernible in the misty spray that hung above the rushing river, sometimes represented as a jumping fish. Like the mist of the waterfall, the Cascayan tends to be elusive. The Cascayan is sometimes misunderstood and their emotions are a mystery. They are highly active and rarely allow themselves to be restricted. Energetic and individual, Cascayans prefer to do things in their own time and their own way, hating to be tied down.

Most Cascayans are sprightly and quick-witted, and many born in this sign share a strong compulsion to keep on the move. Curious by nature, they show considerable interest in their friends' affairs, and are ever ready to help or intercede on behalf of others. They are perhaps the most inquisitive of any sign – Cascayans hate to feel excluded. They are not natural followers, however. Cascayans have an idiosyncratic style all their own.

The Cascayan is a mine of information. Even when they are discussing something of which they have little knowledge, they have the remarkable ability to make it seem as though they are an expert in the field. The Cascayan is eager to impress, and refuses to admit ignorance on any matter. Cascaya is a particularly honest sign – those born in this cycle merely tend to exaggerate. They have a lively imagination and a remarkable talent to make life interesting for everyone.

Positive Characteristics

Cascayans share an active intellect, together with a strong sense of intuition. Self-reliance and determination play an important part in ensuring Cascayan success. Charm and personality arouse the interest of the opposite sex, and music and drama have much appeal. Cascayans have highly energetic personalities, coupled with keen powers of observation. Most are charitable and altruistic, although sometimes eccentric in their ways. There is a marked tendency to lead an unconventional, even Bohemian life-style. Cascayans are fast on the uptake, quick to seize the initiative and are always eager for new experiences.

Negative Characteristics

Often misunderstood, there is sometimes a need for the Cascayan to avoid commitments or responsibilities. Self-sufficiency can sometimes result in alienation from family and relatives. An intense dislike of bureaucracy and a refusal to conform to tradition sometimes results in avoidable complications in the Cascayan's life. Although often gifted with a quick sense of humour, they are inclined to be cynical. Cascayans also lack tact when dealing with those they feel are in the wrong. Intense by nature, Cascayans can be moody or melodramatic at times. Often the Cascayan can be over-inquisitive, which may be disconcerting, even annoying, to some. Many born in this cycle also tend to be too critical of the shortcomings of others.

Appearance

Cascayans of both sexes are usually fast movers. Energetic by temperament, they seldom keep still. Those born in this sign are particularly prone to gesticulating with their hands. Even on the phone, they make exaggerated gestures to emphasize a point or demonstrate what they are saying. Cascayans are restless and fidgety, seldom seeming relaxed. When thinking, they are apt to doodle with a pen or pencil, or else fiddle with matches, pieces of paper or other small objects.

Health

Cascayans are worriers, which may sometimes be detrimental to health. Allergies and ailments related to the nervous system are common complaints for those born in this sign. Not ones for routine, Cascayans have irregular eating habits and often skip meals. The positive effect is that they seldom have a weight problem. Alternatively, such a life-style can play havoc with the digestive system. Cascayans dislike small or confined spaces and may suffer from claustrophobia. They particularly hate elevators or dark and tiny rooms.

The Formula for Success

Cascaya is a sign of communication, and many born in this cycle share a love of language. They are voracious readers, erudite and eloquent, with the ability to express themselves in a vivid and witty manner. They have a marvellous sense of humour although, unlike some signs, it is seldom zany or surreal. Neither is their humour unkind. They are unlikely to appreciate a joke which is at someone else's expense. Cascayans are natural communicators and others may find themselves captivated by their tales and anecdotes. Many Cascayans are excellent speakers with a natural ability to entertain and encourage others. They have an adventurous spirit which often leads them into many unusual situations. Cascayans are at their best when they are the centre of attention, and few born in this sign suffer from stage fright.

Words of Advice

Cascayans are noted for their adaptability and versatility. However, they tend to lack a singleness of purpose, and powers of concentration need deliberate cultivation. Otherwise, even though they have more creative potential than many other signs, they may not make the most of their talents. Cascayans generally spread themselves in too many different directions at one time, and often fail to follow through what they have started. No sooner is something under way, than another, more interesting challenge is eagerly accepted. Cascayans should make longer-term plans – and stick to them.

Suitable Occupations

Cascayans have keen powers of observation and are quick to learn. They are well-suited for occupations that require fast reactions. They are not ideal candidates, however, for work necessitating long periods of intense concentration. They grow restless far too quickly. Teaching appeals to Cascayans, as does anything connected with the media. They are excellent talkers and Cascayans of both sexes are in their element as salespeople. They are not the best of listeners, however, and may fail to realize when they are falling short of persuading a potential buyer. They usually compensate by the sheer volume of work they can accomplish.

Cascayans are happier in the open or away from

headquarters. As white-collar workers they make better travellers, disliking the restrictions of the office environment. Similarly, in manual trades they work best on site. Cascayans can turn their hands to most endeavours, and intricate or inventive work has strong appeal.

The Cascaya at Work

Cascayans can accomplish many tasks simultaneously and are particularly industrious employees. As employers or in a managerial role they make a firm stand on major decisions. On lesser issues they are somewhat changeable, continually updating their strategy. Employees or fellow workers can be left confused by such Cascayan tactics. All the same, their approach is one of adaptability which usually reaps rewards.

As fellow workers they are not always the easiest people to get along with. Some may find Cascayan inquisitiveness annoying. Cascayans are always eager to keep up with gossip and sometimes say more than they should. Alternatively, they can be tremendous fun to be around, making the most laborious activities seem interesting.

The Cascaya Woman

In general, the Cascayan woman makes a better sweetheart than a wife. She may be a devoted lover, but she finds household chores bothersome. She has no intention of spending hours washing, cleaning or preparing meals, although she will warmly welcome visitors to her home. Her usual response is 'take me as you find me'. The Cascayan woman refuses to play the submissive wife. She will often insist on helping with the income, and is happiest when she is a wage earner.

Although somewhat untidy, she will treat her home as an efficient business, ensuring that the accounts are kept well in order.

As a career woman, the Cascayan is a conscientious worker. She is a marvellous organizer of business affairs, although somewhat sloppy, leaving everything lying around. Her desk is usually piled high with notes and other pieces of paper – a constant reminder of her busy schedule. Because the Cascayan can easily handle numerous tasks simultaneously, many women born in this sign will continue with their chosen occupation once their children have reached school age. Most Cascayans also expect their partners to share the responsibility of child-caring.

When it comes to choosing clothes, Cascayan women especially like suits and separates, which they excel at teaming together. They are also born in the sign that most likes jewellery. Bracelets, rings, chains, earrings and brooches – the Cascayan woman loves them to excess.

The Cascaya Man

The Cascayan man has a boyish air that is particularly attractive to the opposite sex. He is considerate to women and treats them as equals. Most Cascayan men fall for women with strong personalities, sometimes much older than themselves.

Cascayan men have plenty of charm. They can turn it on at will and are generous with their compliments. They are gifted with a quick or dry sense of humour and are always ready with a witty or pertinent remark. They usually share a frivolous attitude to life. When annoyed, however, they can be extremely sarcastic. Indeed, this is their usual means of defence. As a rule, the Cascayan is a peace lover and is unlikely to resort to violence. Indeed, they are so expert with their tongues that few Cascayan men have need to succumb to fist fights or brawls. They do have a temper, however, but are inclined to take it out on the furniture or other inanimate objects. It is usually the Cascayan man who smashes a plate or snaps a pencil when he has reached the end of his tether. Cascayans find a noisy way to express their anger, which accordingly releases tension.

Cascayans are somewhat untidy – Cascayan men in particular. However, they always know precisely where everything is. If you tidy up after a Cascayan man it can throw his life into turmoil. 'Now I don't know where anything is,' he is often heard to complain.

The Cascaya Parent

Cascayans are perhaps the most exciting parents for any child. They just love to be involved with their children's games. They wholeheartedly join in the fun, and are forever dreaming up adventurous pastimes for their young. Holidays, in particular, can be full of adventure. The Cascayan mother is young at heart and goes out of her way to follow her daughter's fashion – at least, as far as it is feasible. The Cascayan father similarly takes a keen interest in his son's activities; sharing a fishing trip or a visit to a ball game is a common joy for many men born in this sign. Sometimes children of a Cascayan may find themselves embarrassed by their parent's enthusiasm, especially in front of their friends.

The Cascaya Child

Children born in this cycle are quick to learn, particularly to read. At school, Cascayans are often remarkable achievers, although they can be a bane for teachers. There will be few complaints concerning academic ability, but school reports may repeatedly criticize the Cascayan's lack of concentration. The problem for many Cascayan children is that they have usually understood the lesson early on, but grow restless and irritable whilst waiting for the other children to catch up. The Cascayan is a worrier and consequently examination results may suffer. As they are exceptionally keen to do well, children of this sign often overtax themselves on homework.

Cascayans are likely to succeed in life much earlier than many other signs. Indeed, many a child prodigy is born in this cycle. Their success in later life, however, depends very much upon controlling their inclination to chop and change the nature of their work. Cascayans find it hard to stick to anything for long, especially once it has become a matter of familiar routine.

The Cascaya Friend

The Cascayan just hates to pass up a challenge, and will often bypass all commitments to pursue a new opportunity. Strangely enough, those born in this cycle are the first to draw attention to the inconsistency of others. The Cascayan is particularly critical of the changing moods of the Oryx, or the adaptability of the Phoenix. Another handicap for the Cascayan is a tendency to become embroiled in petty details. Once more, they share such characteristics with the Oryx, but are quick to draw attention to the Oryx's fussy behaviour. Do not try arguing with a Cascayan, however; it will get you nowhere – except into a state of confusion. The Cascayan will have you skilfully sidetracked, just when you think you have proved a point.

Cascayans enjoy numerous acquaintances but fewer long-standing friendships. One or two particularly close friends is usually their limit. With these few

friends, the Cascayan love of language and gossip
makes them eager to keep in touch. Cascayans can
spend a fortune on writing paper, stamps and phone
calls.

Occasionally Cascayans show signs of jealousy, but
this is usually only skin-deep. With frequently changing interests, they are quick to forget. If you seem to
have offended the Cascayan, you may be inclined to
formulate a strategy to apologize. It usually isn't worth
the bother. The Cascayan has probably forgotten all
about it. The best attitude to adopt with most
Cascayans is live and let live.

The Cascaya Partner

Others will always know when the Cascayan is
annoyed. Partners will notice how they move noisily
around the house, banging furniture or slamming
doors. When a river is in flood the waterfall is anything
but silent.

Sometimes Cascayans form deep attachments, at
others they move from one relationship to another with
considerable ease. It may seem that they will never
settle down; then suddenly, out of the blue, they
announce they are about to marry. Generally, once the
choice is made, they will work hard to ensure a lasting
partnership; that is provided their partner is prepared to
accommodate the Cascayan's manifold interests. If a
partner strongly disagrees with a Cascayan's activities,
the ideal strategy is to give it time. Before long, they
usually find something else to do and quickly lose
interest in the previous activity.

Cascayans hate to be pressured. The best way to
handle a Cascayan is to air your objections and let the
subject drop. At first they will strongly disagree, then,
some time later, you will probably find them doing

exactly what you wanted, while giving the impression
that it was their intention all along. Just leave them with
that belief – Cascayans hate it to appear as though they
have been influenced or proved wrong.

Cascayans relish an evening out, and with every
romantic detail. Both Cascayan men and women excel
at dinner-table conversation, and both love to buy their
partners presents. The Cascayan is one of the best signs
with whom to share a date. In domestic life they can be
somewhat irritating, however. They can never make
up their minds about the colour of wallpaper or a new
model of car. Even when they finally decide, they are
forever complaining – if only they had chosen
differently.

Affinity Signs

The Swallow: Many born in the Swallow sign are calm
and serene, well able to take the highly-charged
Cascayan in their stride.

The Griffin: Griffins are usually prepared to give others
their own space – something the Cascayan desperately
needs. Unlike some signs, the Griffin is usually an
open book, having no problem with Cascayan
inquisitiveness.

Etana: Both signs are particularly tolerant of one
another. The Etana's shortcomings are similar to the
Cascayan's own, such as escaping from tiresome
responsibilities whenever possible. Both hate to be tied
down.

Cascaya: With so many interests, Cascayans seldom
find themselves in conflict with other Cascayans.

Problem Signs

The Oryx: The Oryx values privacy too much to be constantly around the Cascayan. The Cascayan often finds fault with Oryx changeability. Cascayans are themselves changeable, but in interests and activities and not, as the Oryx, in temperament.

The Huntress: Like the Oryx, Huntresses need their own space. The Cascayan intends to be a part of everything – too much so for the Huntress' liking.

The Assari: The Assari is far too sentimental for the Cascayan, as Assaris seek close relationships and have a need for firm commitments. The adventurous Cascayan feels far too restricted by such demands.

The Sphinx: The meticulous Sphinx can be most annoying to the Cascayan. The two signs have markedly different temperaments and little in common.

Other Signs

The Genie: Genii are romantics and the Cascayan loves anything adventurous. Many Genii make an eager audience for the charm and wit of the Cascayan.

The Serpent: Serpents and Cascayans mix well enough socially, although close relationships are rare. Serpents are much too pragmatic for Cascayans.

The Dragon: Dragons like to commit themselves to long-term endeavours. The Cascayan is quickly irritated with anything that becomes routine or lacks variety.

The Phoenix: Phoenixes and Cascayans usually work

well together, although in relationships the Phoenix seeks consistency generally lacking in the Cascayan life.

The Hero: The Hero and the Cascayan often have many common interests. However, Cascayans hate to be ordered around or told what to do. The Hero is sometimes too authoritative for the Cascayan's liking.

Famous Cascayans

Michael Caine. Born: 14 March 1933.

Many women find Cascayan men lovable – the sort they want to mother. Michael Caine has a certain vulnerability about him, so often evident in the Cascayan male. Cascaya is a sign of industrious optimism, and whenever he is on screen Michael Caine always appears fresh, alert and in good humour. The perfect entertainer, as a quick-thinking Cascayan he is always ready with a witty and pertinent remark. Like many born in this sign, Michael Caine has a cool, highly individual sense of humour.

David Frost. Born: 7 April 1939.

Cascaya is a sign of vigour, and David Frost exudes a contagious area of enthusiasm. Cascayans are very much individualists, with their own way of doing things. Primarily, it is David's idiosyncratic style which has made him unique amongst the media personalities of the world. Many born in the cycle of Cascaya are industrious and hard-working, with keen powers of observation. All these Cascayan attributes are utilized by David as one of Britain's best known interviewers. Many Cascayans are gifted with a dry sense of humour, a trait for which David Frost is renowned.

Liza Minnelli. Born: 12 March 1946.

Liza has tremendous charisma and like many Cascayans she is not inclined to hide her views and beliefs. Many Cascayans are excellent communicators with a natural ability to encourage those about them. Liza uses her sense of humour to overcome adversity and to help others see the funny side of almost anything. Not only is Liza a born entertainer, she can draw upon a wide variety of personal experiences. Like most Cascayans, her adventurous spirit has led her into many unique situations. Cascaya is a sign of multifarious artistic talent. As a singer, dancer and actress, Liza is the epitome of the successful Cascayan.

Fate and Fortune

Over the course of the year Cascayans can expect the following influences to affect their lives during the separate lunar cycles:

Cascaya: During their own month Cascayans should be careful not to overwork. It is a time when haste could jeopardize business affairs or result in errors of judgement concerning finances. In matters of love and romance, however, the Cascayan may be pleasantly surprised.

The Phoenix: Cascaya is a sign of mercurial energy. The Phoenix is also a sign of rapidity, bringing progress for many Cascayans.

The Hero: The Hero is a sign of achievement in material affairs. It is a sign of steady progress – requiring patience – and patience is not a Cascayan virtue.

Cascayans should not give up if something seems hopeless or slow in development. There is probably far more headway being made than they realize.

Assari: Cascayans may find themselves entangled in quarrels or experience difficulty in relationships during the Assari month.

The Genie: This is usually a month of reward for a Cascayan. The Genie is a sign of romantic adventure and the Cascayan craves change and variety. New scope is often recognized by Cascayans at this time. An opportunity grasped during this cycle can often lead to great success. It is also a positive month for any Cascayan seeking a new romantic affiliation.

The Griffin: The Griffin month can be a time of intense activity for Cascayans. They are more single-minded than at any other time of the year.

The Oryx: The Oryx is a sign of swift activity, while Cascaya is a sign of quick thinking. As both are highly changeable by nature, the Cascayan should be careful of making snap decisions.

Etana: Etana is a sign of risk and courage, favourable for Cascayan speculation. This is a month of adventure for the Cascayan, and affairs of the heart can move in a positive direction. This is also a time of advantageous meetings and important new acquaintances.

The Serpent: Plans for change are best implemented during this cycle. Any Cascayan seeking a new job or change of location may discover exciting possibilities.

The Dragon: Water extinguishes fire and fire dries water. The influence of the fire-breathing Dragon has a tendency to evaporate the positive influences of the watery Cascaya. Plans can be dashed and hopes and aspirations may seem to fade. The Cascayan should tread carefully in domestic affairs; an innocent remark could be taken the wrong way.

The Sphinx: An intriguing mystery may confront the Cascayan during the month of the riddle-guarding Sphinx. The Sphinx may also bring financial reward. It is a particularly lucky month for Cascayans, especially concerning games or sporting activities.

The Swallow: The month of the high-flying Swallow is often a time of travel for the Cascayan. It is a good month for a vacation or weekend away. It is also a time for favourable news.

The Huntress: For those born in any sign, the intermittent Huntress month is often a time for the unusual or unexpected. A word of warning, however – the Cascayan should avoid taking everything at face value.

THE PHOENIX

Approximate Calendar Month
. APRIL

Sign Chart Letter
B

THE PHOENIX

IN legend this exotic bird made its nest of spices, and when the sun's rays set it alight the Phoenix was burned to cinders. A few days later a new Phoenix was born, rising majestically from the ashes of the old. The main characteristic of those born in the sign of the Phoenix is the ability to create possibilities from very little. They are optimistic in the extreme, seldom accepting anything as hopeless. Usually able to find some good even in their worst enemies, the Phoenix is remarkably resilient. Perhaps the best phrase to describe their attitudes is 'where there's a will there's a way'. They have a close affinity with nature and are often conservationists; ecology and the plight of animals are important priorities for the Phoenix. Possessed with a wide range of skills, the Phoenix can be a 'Jack of all trades', seeking practical applications for their talents.

Travel has enormous appeal for the Phoenix, who usually likes secluded places. Hot climates are preferred – winter holidays are not for them. Born in the sign of the firebird, the Phoenix dislikes the cold intensely. Conversely, they can function well in even the worst of heat waves, rushing around busily while others are sweltering. Hot or spicy foods are also a favourite for the Phoenix.

Preferring to be active, watching general television programmes or casual reading are not high on the Phoenix list of priorities. The exceptions are sport or game shows, which the Phoenix may follow with zeal. Musical tastes are somewhat deep, for it is often the meaning of a song rather than the tune which is important to the Phoenix.

Positive Characteristics

Resilient, optimistic and determined, the Phoenix possesses an inventive and adaptable personality. They are industrious and highly active, with the ability to find new uses for the most unlikely things. Technically-gifted in the crafts, the Phoenix also has a conscientious attitude to work. There is a strong tendency to champion the plight of the unfortunate, and an enviable power to inspire confidence and enthusiasm in others.

Negative Characteristics

The Phoenix has a stubborn streak. They prefer to do things their own way – even when they know they are wrong. Often a dreamer, the Phoenix may refuse to face reality when problems occur. Too much time is spent on failed endeavours, when the best course of action would be to move on to something else. The Phoenix is often headstrong and occasionally egotistical.

Appearance

Those born in this sign often have a determined appearance. Their intensive eyes are extremely attractive to the opposite sex. The Phoenix's nose is usually sharp, although the chin tends to be round. Weight is seldom a problem; an abundance of nervous energy generally keeps the Phoenix slim and agile. Many born in this sign have a cheeky demeanour. Phoenix men may have a rugged look, while the Phoenix woman often has a mischievous smile.

Health

The Phoenix usually enjoys good health, although skin complaints may be a problem. More often than not, this is the result of stress. Diet is seldom a cause of concern for the Phoenix. They can eat almost anything without ill-effect. Back problems may be in evidence due to a tendency to stoop. Like the Oryx, the Phoenix is a sign of good health and those born in this cycle are usually fit and trim.

The Formula for Success

The Phoenix has tremendous vitality. Life is an adventure for the Phoenix, although a craving for excitement may lead to tricky situations. Always eager for new experiences, and ready to rise to the challenge, the Phoenix's life is full of surprises. So much do they endeavour to fill their lives with excitement, sometimes they forget about the smaller, more practical matters of life. Others may be content to wait for opportunities to arise; Phoenixes will create their own. Indeed, they consider it their personal responsibility to seek out new and interesting possibilities. Two words can describe the Phoenix's strongest attributes; initiative and enterprise. They are never at a loss for something to do. Most born in the cycle have many talents that they can utilize simultaneously.

Words of Advice

Once Phoenixes have made up their minds, they are firm in their convictions. The Phoenix, however, is a sign of action rather than words, and handling a skilled debate is something they find hard. When faced with opposition, the Phoenix generally loses patience, brushing off adverse opinion with an exasperating shrug. Few Phoenixes spend time consulting with others, and are apt to jump to conclusions far too quickly. They sometimes lack sound judgement, although they more than compensate by an abundance of will-power.

Most problems the Phoenix encounters arise from an inability to see things from someone else's point of view. Although they are sympathetic to those in obvious distress, they are usually so wrapped up in their own affairs that they take little interest in the opinions of others. Phoenixes should listen to those around them before arriving at conclusions.

Suitable Occupations
With an adventurous temperament, the Phoenix is especially suited for hazardous occupations. Whether manual or white-collar workers, Phoenixes are generally most successful when self-employed. Few Phoenixes work well with money, so financial careers are best left to others. Phoenix enthusiasm is contagious and a career in sales or promotion can be highly successful. Technically-gifted, those born in this sign make excellent mechanics and engineers.

The Phoenix at Work
Happiest when working alone, the Phoenix is unlikely to make a success of a business partnership. In any working environment, if colleagues are prepared to let the Phoenix do things their own way positive results often follow. Phoenixes make tough but fair employers, although they may drive their employees a little too hard.

As an employee, Phoenix optimism is always a valuable contribution to any workforce. Sometimes, however, their optimism may prove frustrating, particularly if an enterprise is an obvious failure. The Phoenix just doesn't know when to quit. Phoenixes are imaginative and creative but lack foresight. Unfortunately, when in the wrong they can be stubborn to the extreme. They find it hard to change or adapt to new situations which are not of their choosing.

The Phoenix is an active sign and few born in this cycle are patient by nature. Their answer to most difficulties is to simply get started and meet problems head-on. Driving force, self-assurance and ambition are strong Phoenix traits, and most are usually ahead in the rat race.

The Phoenix Woman

The self-reliant Phoenix makes an excellent career woman. If a housewife, she will probably need an outside interest. Invariably, the Phoenix woman is at her best when dividing her talents equally between domestic and business affairs. Possessing an abundance of energy, she can easily handle both.

The Phoenix woman has a masculine streak and often prefers the company of men. Phoenix femininity is more commanding than sensual, although there is no lack of romance in her life. As most Phoenix women are able to hold their own in a male environment, a man's reaction is either one of admiration or irritation. Few can simply take-or-leave a Phoenix woman. Her individualism can lead to problems if a partner expects her to remain passive and pretty. Alternatively, if he is prepared to take the relationship on an equal footing, life can be fulfilling for both.

The Phoenix woman is seldom jealous. If her partner

appears interested in someone else, she usually knows precisely what to do. If she fails, her response is generally 'he's not worth the bother'. Her partner is expected to work at the relationship – if he fails her, the Phoenix woman will soon look elsewhere. In love, as in most areas of her life, if something is not working out she is inclined to make a clean break and quickly start again.

High fashion is unimportant to the Phoenix woman, although she has excellent dress sense. She wears the right clothes for the right occasions. Dress sense comes naturally and friends seek her advice. Most clothes suit the Phoenix woman; she looks just as good in jeans and a T-shirt as in the most elaborate evening wear.

The Phoenix Man

The Phoenix is more accident-prone than many signs, often due to haste rather than carelessness. Unfortunately, the Phoenix man is usually more hasty than his female counterpart. Although he is often preoccupied with the safety of others, he tends to disregard such precautions himself. The Phoenix is a skilled craftsman and will usually attempt to rectify a household fault himself, before calling an expert. Stubbornly, when the problem is beyond his ability, he refuses to quit, only to make things worse.

The Phoenix man is impossible to drag away from anything he is involved in, and needs repeatedly to be called to meals. If he is doing the cooking, however, it's another story. The Phoenix man is the first to lose patience when someone else is late. Wildly enthusiastic about whoever or whatever is the focus of his attention, the Phoenix is oblivious to anyone or anything else.

Most Phoenixes love sport, games or competitions. The Phoenix man, however, is not the best for team events, finding it hard to work in close harmony with others. On the other hand, the Phoenix can make a good team leader. So long as team-mates follow orders, the Phoenix is prepared to make any personal sacrifice to assure success.

Phoenix men lack grace and are seldom good dancers. If the Phoenix takes to the dance floor – watch out!

The Phoenix Parent

Phoenix parents usually expect their children to share their own interests, and are often disappointed in this respect. They look after their children well but sometimes expect too much. They are rather too eager to tell them how to run their lives. Phoenix parents are not strict or overbearing by nature – they just want their children to be like them.

Phoenixes are usually concerned parents and offer their children much encouragement. The Phoenix mother is especially proud of her sons, but may find it difficult to relate to her daughters. This is especially true once they reach adolescence. They are too ready to offer their own advice on teenage life. Conversely, the Phoenix man will spoil his daughters, while being a little too hard on his sons. Both, however, bring up all their children with pride.

The Phoenix Child

In legend the Phoenix was reborn in the heart of the desert. Like the firebird, Phoenix children are happy to spend time in seclusion. They are certainly not shy or reclusive, but are content to play alone.

The Phoenix child can be a handful for parents and teachers alike. Right from infancy, Phoenixes make it very clear they have a will of their own. Boisterous in play, they may be given to tantrums if they fail to get their own way. They are at their best when given liberty to think and act for themselves.

The competitive Phoenix spirit emerges in childhood, and most children born in this sign are keen to do well. Although many are good at sport, few succeed in team games. Individual events are best for the Phoenix child, who often excels at athletics or swimming. Phoenix children are not particularly good at taking care of their possessions and a careless streak can result in many a broken toy.

The Phoenix boy is unafraid to tackle a child older or bigger than himself. Sometimes this leads to brawls. The Phoenix girl is a tomboy, preferring the company of boys to other girls. Always keen to show she can do anything as well as they, cuts, bruises and dirty clothes are often the result. She will have outgrown her dolls at an early age, and if she has a brother it is his toys with which she prefers to play. Like the Phoenix boy, she enjoys sport, but domestic science and needlework are subjects she will often despise.

In youth, Phoenixes have many relationships with the opposite sex. Mostly, however, they are platonic, which others may find difficult to accept. When they are prepared for a romantic commitment, it is usually later in life.

The Phoenix Friend

The Phoenix is one of the most robust of signs and those born in this cycle have resilient personalities. They will not let the opinions of others deter or influence their actions, ignoring sneers or cruel remarks if something has failed.

Courageous by nature, Phoenixes are always ready to take risks for their friends. The Phoenix is good in a crisis, usually the first to suggest a solution. Even if something seems hopeless, the Phoenix is excellent at keeping things calm. In times of peril the Phoenix will endanger themselves for the good of others, and in war they are often those decorated for feats of heroism.

Although they see the best in most people, Phoenixes dislike arrogance and hate aggression. They are kind and sympathetic to those who are shy or in distress; it is often the Phoenix who comes to the aid of those in trouble. Phoenixes make excellent companions for anyone prepared to take a back seat now and again. They are never boring to be around, but their need for occasional solitude can sometimes be taken the wrong way.

The Phoenix Partner

Phoenixes will speak their minds frankly, making their motives and objectives clear. Most signs know where they stand with the Phoenix. Tact is not a Phoenix attribute, however, and those of this sign tend to be forthright and outspoken. They seldom lose their temper, although irritability is the usual Phoenix response to someone who has failed to understand their motives. Phoenixes sometimes say more than is wise, and find it difficult to apologize if they have offended without intent. Their usual form of apology is to make up for it in some way without ever saying they are actually sorry.

Not particularly sensual in love, the Phoenix may appear restrained in a relationship. However, they are kind and generous. The Phoenix may be a passionate lover, but romantic small talk is beyond their scope.

Because of their impetuous nature, the Phoenix can fall in love at first sight. They seldom dwell too long on any decision. Actions speak louder than words for the lover born in this sign, and many rush too readily into marriage. So long as the choice is right, however, relationships can be long-lasting. Phoenixes make ideal partners as they hate domestic strife. They would rather give way to their partner's demands than create a fuss. There is usually too much else on their minds for them to become entangled in a quarrel.

Affinity Signs

The Swallow: The Phoenix gets on best with those who are less active than themselves. Many born in the Swallow sign are calm and serene – at least outwardly. Accordingly, they can exert a positive influence on the Phoenix's impulsive nature.

The Huntress: In legend, once reborn, the Phoenix was impelled to fly to the temple of Heliopolis. Like the mythical bird, those born in the Phoenix sign will find themselves attracted to the exotic or unusual. The Huntress is perhaps the most intriguing of signs, and their idiosyncratic style is irresistible to the Phoenix.

The Oryx: Oryxes are mood-swingers and their behaviour can be erratic. Unlike many signs, the Phoenix is almost impervious to the emotional swings of others. As both the Phoenix and the Oryx need their own space, they make excellent partners and long-lasting relationships are possible.

The Genie and Assari: Like the Oryx, the Phoenix particularly likes the company of the Genie and Assari. Both have a romantic temperament which the Phoenix finds inspiring.

Problem Signs

Etana: Potentially the most problematic for the Phoenix is the Etana. The Phoenix can recover from most failures, but the Etana finds it hard. Both signs are adventurous, but when the Phoenix burned to ashes it rose again. The two signs interact well to begin with, but should problems occur the Phoenix cannot understand the Etana's inability to cope.

The Hero and the Serpent: The Serpent and the Hero are generally signs where the Phoenix finds difficulty. Both leadership signs, they enjoy taking charge far too much for the Phoenix's liking.

Other Signs

Cascaya: Phoenixes and Cascayans usually work well together, although in relationships the Phoenix usually seeks consistency.

The Dragon: Both the Dragon and the Phoenix are signs of extreme optimism, and the two get on like a house on fire; after all, they are both creatures of fire. Unfortunately, the restraining element of other signs is needed by both. When alone together the Phoenix and the Dragon can find themselves in adverse situations which are difficult to remedy.

The Phoenix: Two Phoenixes work well together but, like the Dragon, problems can arise through too little care or planning.

The Griffin: Phoenixes find Griffins too pragmatic. These signs seldom mix well as close companions, although on a superficial level there are few problems.

The Sphinx: The Phoenix dislike of financial matters is

well-compensated for by the Sphinx. The Sphinx is both conservative and thrifty in approach to most endeavours, and the Phoenix respects such attributes in others.

Famous Phoenixes

Shirley MacLaine. Born: 24 April 1934.

Like the exotic Phoenix, those born in this sign can rise majestically from the ashes of adversity. Shirley MacLaine well demonstrates this Phoenix resilience, often creating unique opportunities for herself against a background of difficulty. Seldom seeing anything as hopeless, Shirley pursues her career with positive direction and continual optimism. She shares the energetic influences of this cycle, having both a lively personality and an enthusiastic demeanour. Typically Phoenix, she is a natural survivor and has continued to enjoy international recognition for many years. Phoenix multi-talented characteristics are exhibited by Shirley who has been both a successful straight and comedy actress, a writer, lecturer and a popular personality the world over. Many Phoenixes are fascinated by the mysterious or mystical side of life, and Shirley's interest in the paranormal is typical of those born in this cycle.

Jack Nicholson. Born: 28 April 1937.

The vitality of the energetic Phoenix is aptly demonstrated by the sheer power of a Jack Nicholson performance. Like most born in this sign, his presence never fails to make an impact. The commitment and determination with which he handles his roles has made him a Hollywood legend. The Phoenix possesses tremendous will-power and concentration, able to envelope themselves completely in whatever they are doing. Typically, Jack will build himself up for hours to play a particularly demanding scene. With Phoenix tunnel vision, he is completely absorbed in the part. Those born in this cycle have a fascination with anything out-of-the-ordinary and are invariably drawn to the unusual. No wonder Jack Nicholson should so often play characters who are so bizarre.

Dudley Moore. Born: 19 April 1935.

The Phoenix is a sign of vitality, determination and energy. Like many born in this sign, Dudley Moore has an ample share of all three, having excelled in so many different respects. One of the world's most versatile performers, he is an accomplished musician, a television comedian and a big-screen actor. Few can boast such a varied career. Dudley has been a popular jazz pianist with his Dudley Moore Trio, one of Britain's best-loved comedians in his partnership with Peter Cook, and ultimately one of Hollywood's star attractions. Dudley has the typically cheeky attitude of the Phoenix man, and his bubbly personality is a favourite with women the world over.

Fate and Fortune

Over the course of the year Phoenixes can expect the following influences to affect their lives during the separate lunar cycles:

Cascaya: Romantic disappointments are possible, although it is a particularly favourable month for financial affairs. New opportunities often arise during the Cascayan month for the Phoenix, while long-standing projects may end. This is very much a month of change.

The Phoenix: Some signs fare well during their own month and the Phoenix is one such sign. It is a favourable time for travel, change of location or employment. Good news, especially by mail, can be expected.

The Hero: A combination of the assertive Hero and the determined Phoenix is favourable for business matters. It is a time of especially good fortune in financial affairs. It is not, however, a particularly romantic period for the Phoenix. Difficulties in relationships are possible due to distractions and preoccupations.

Assari: As a sign of air, the Assari month can bring much activity to the Phoenix. As wind feeds the flames, Assari brings energy to the Phoenix. During this cycle the Phoenix should try to keep their imagination under control. There is a tendency to forge ahead far too quickly. A cautious approach to most endeavours is advised. Any Phoenix seeking love or romance, however, may be pleasantly surprised at this time of the year.

The Genie: For the Phoenix, the Genie month can be a time of relative tranquillity. Few Phoenixes are quiet or reserved by nature, and impatience may result. Many Phoenixes will find themselves especially frustrated by humdrum, everyday events. This is a good time to take a break. Vacations and leisure activities are favourably placed.

The Griffin: During this month, love, romance and affairs of the heart are favourably placed for the

Phoenix. In new relationships it is an especially adventurous period. For longer-standing partnerships, it may be time for more permanent commitments to be considered.

The Oryx: The magical Oryx brings imaginative and fresh ideas to the Phoenix mind. New notions conceived during this month are likely to be well-founded. At this time of the year the Phoenix tends to make sound decisions.

Etana: The Phoenix should be more careful during the Etana month than at any other time. Both are signs of risks taken courageously. The Etana will walk where angels fear to treat, while the Phoenix has little fear of failure. Combined, these influences are apt to leave the Phoenix wide open to rash decisions.

The Serpent: As a sign of wisdom, the Serpent will balance Phoenix impetuousness. This can be an especially favourable time for complicated matters, previously unresolved. Sporting activities are particularly favoured for the Phoenix during this month. Surprise news can also be expected.

The Dragon: Both the Phoenix and the Dragon are creatures of fire. During this month Phoenix imagination will be at its most effective. Most projects are likely to succeed due to the quick reactions of the Phoenix. Relationships or friendships may suffer, however, as the Phoenix may be particularly argumentative at this time of year.

The Sphinx: The Sphinx month can be a period of stagnation for the Phoenix. If things do not seem to be moving ahead as quickly as the Phoenix hoped, matters should be given a little more time.

The Swallow: Very often Phoenixes will be in their element during a Swallow month. Normal practical restraints will be lifted by the influence of the high-flying Swallow; the firebird is free to soar to new heights. Romantic, financial and leisure activities are all favourably placed. This is a month of good luck in matters of chance or lottery.

The Huntress: For most signs the Huntress month can be filled with unforeseen events. The Phoenix should be prepared for an unexpected meeting with an old acquaintance. This may open a completely new chapter in the Phoenix's life.

THE HERO

Approximate Calendar Month
MAY

Sign Chart Letter
C

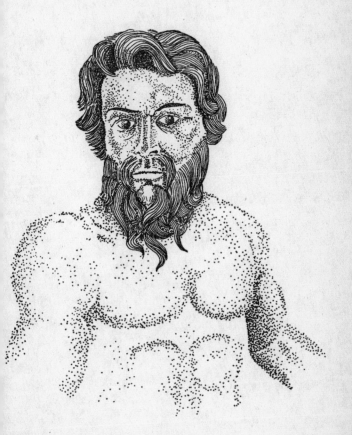

THE HERO

LIKE the ancient hero Gilgamesh, those born in this sign are strong and resolute, others looking to them for guidance. The Hero, however, can often fail to understand those less strong, finding it incomprehensible that the tasks they find easy, others may find hard. They make excellent leaders so long as they remember not to overtax their followers. Although not lacking imagination, Heroes generally feel that lofty ideas stand in the way of solid business. At their best in difficult situations, the appropriate phrase to epitomize the Hero would be: 'When the going gets tough, the tough get going'. Alternatively, if left without a challenge the Hero may lapse into a state of lethargy, content to watch the world go by. They are not the best people in the world to initiate a project, although, once under way, Hero leadership traits afford an invaluable contribution towards success.

Particularly conscientious in most endeavours, the Hero often plays a leading role in political organizations or social groups. Few born in this sign are inclined to do anything on the spur of the moment and most are averse to change. The Hero forms firm opinions and convictions; they are perhaps the most principled of any sign. Anything to which the Hero's mind is set is well within the realms of possibility. They have a practical attitude to life and are seldom ones for dreaming, reminiscing or fantasizing. The Hero is a realist and most born in this cycle have an abundance of common sense.

Positive Characteristics

Heroes have exceptional powers of leadership and a strong will is matched by excellent executive skills. With considerable ability for making money, the Hero is always willing to devote time and effort towards the success of an enterprise. Strongly principled, they often possess great courage and are reliable and trustworthy. With a vital personality, they usually enjoy robust health, coupled with a love of sport, action and outdoor activities.

Negative Characteristics

An overbearing attitude may reduce the chances of social success, while a headstrong temperament, matched by intolerance, can lead to conflict. Errors of judgement are sometimes made due to strongly-biased opinions. Many Heroes share unrealistic expectations of others, and stubborn adherence to ideas can make certain relationships difficult. Sometimes the Hero can be arrogant, even demonstrative.

Appearance

Those born in this sign are often sturdy in appearance, have firm features and share a confident and authoritative stature. The Hero usually looks you straight in the eyes while exuding a powerful countenance. In youth the Hero male is usually broad-shouldered or muscular, and the female curvaceous. However, although this is a sign of activity, it is not a sign of nervous energy. There may therefore be a tendency towards overweight, particularly in later life.

Health

Throat infections are common for those born in this sign, especially in childhood, when frequent bouts of tonsillitis are common. As the Hero is a physically active sign, injuries and broken limbs are frequent amongst this group. Some signs may be slim, even skinny, no matter what their lifestyle. The Hero, however, needs to make a concerted effort regarding diet or exercise to remain trim.

The Formula for Success

The Hero is an especially patient sign, and most Heroes apply themselves with continued diligence to any enterprise. In business matters Heroes make excellent spokespeople, able to negotiate the best of bargains. The Hero, however, is not the ideal sign for initiating a new project, being suspicious of the risks involved. Experimentation is not a Hero trait, and most born in this sign are reluctant gamblers. Heroes prefer to keep their feet firmly on the ground. Having excellent administrative ability, it is often the Hero who is the most suitable leader in sporting events, or manager in business affairs. They are capable organizers and keep a firm grip on financial matters. Moreover, they are always ready to assume command and are unafraid when it comes to exercising authority or making important decisions.

Words of Advice

Heroes are often over-cautious and share a stubborn reluctance to take chances. They may be highly competent organisers and administrators, but experimentation and risk-taking is best left to others. Sometimes their hesitance can be a handicap; frequently they fail to exploit their capabilities or realize their full

potential. They often become set in their ways, finding
it difficult to adapt to new situations. For the best
results, the Hero should learn to take the occasional
risk, and realize that failures are often an important part
of learning.

Suitable Occupations

Heroes prefer occupations offering steady advancement and long-term security. Their enviable patience
sees them through times of difficulty, usually leading to
supervisory or managerial roles in their chosen line of
work. Those born in this cycle are good with money,
so financial careers have considerable appeal. Heroes
make excellent bankers, although work involving
financial speculation is not the forte of the cautious
Hero.

Heroes are usually successful in whatever occupation
they choose. They make sensible and responsible
decisions in management and are conscientious
workers. The Hero is a versatile sign regarding
employment and most born in this cycle are quite
capable of learning almost any trade.

The Hero at Work

The Hero is a sign of fixed character; few born in this
cycle have adaptable personalities. If a change in outlook or direction is required in their working
environment, the Hero may find it hard to adapt.
Heroes are consistent in outlooks, habits and
behaviour, and pursue a professional objective with
continued application and dedication. They make the
most steadfast of colleagues and fellow workers
generally know exactly where they stand with the
Hero.

As employers, Heroes are especially aware of the

needs and abilities of those for whom they are responsible. They do, however, expect others to commit themselves to an enterprise with as much dedication as themselves. As an employee, the Hero is an industrious worker, although they do not necessarily mix well with their colleagues. They are easy enough to get along with during working hours, but Heroes like to draw a strict dividing line between working and social life. Often their personal friends are from an entirely separate circle of acquaintances.

The Hero Woman

The Hero is both an industrious career woman and a committed housewife. Unlike some signs, however, she may find difficulty mixing the two. The happiest Hero is often she who has devoted her life to one or the other. Most Heroes dislike consistently having to change hats during the course of their life. In work and in home life alike, the Hero woman enjoys organization, making her the perfect hostess. She is keen to ensure that everything runs smoothly during social occasions and commits herself accordingly.

The Hero's home is uncluttered, practical and clean. Furnishings are often modern rather than antique, and ornamentation is kept to a minimum. The exception is floral decoration. Her home is usually well-furnished with cacti and other indoor plants. The garden is also important to the Hero woman, and it is usually impeccably kept. She prefers to do the gardening herself, rather than let her partner disturb the order and symmetry she has painstakingly created.

The Hero woman can be a trendy dresser, certain to be wearing the latest middle-of-the-road style: nothing outrageous or unusual. Those born in this sign like to feel secure in their surroundings, so the Hero always looks the part. Uneasy if standing out in a crowd, she will wear what is the majority fashion for her peer group.

The Hero woman will take a central role in social activities. She is always ready to give advice and is often the best shoulder on which to cry. Her own problems, however, she keeps to herself, being the last to worry others with her own concerns. Outwardly, she may seem unemotional; it is so difficult to tell what the Hero woman is really thinking or, more importantly, how she is feeling. Like her male counterpart, unless angered, the Hero woman keeps her emotions very much to herself.

The Hero Man

The Hero man is brave and courageous, usually in command of most situations. Circumstances where he might experience difficulty he usually avoids from the outset. He is confident in character, consistent in behaviour and in his response to most problems he is calm, controlled and effective. However, like the woman of this sign, Hero men have a nasty temper if pushed too far.

The Hero undertakes most activities in a precise and methodical way. A man of regular habits, the Hero is the last person to cause surprise with uncharacteristic behaviour. Although he may be somewhat predictable, he is good-humoured in most situations and an excellent conversationalist. With the opposite sex he is always the perfect gentlemen and his manners are impeccable.

The Hero is not a man to make large numbers of casual acquaintances; a small circle of close friends is preferred. He is disturbed by company not of his choosing, and often prefers to attend social functions with his own acquaintances rather than his partner's circle of friends. Accordingly, Hero wives sometimes find themselves isolated in marriage. Another problem for Hero wives can be the mother-in-law. Hero men often remain extremely attached to their mothers, sometimes allowing them to influence their lives a little too much for their partners' liking.

Like his female counterpart, the Hero man keeps a strict account of his money and economizes whenever possible. All the same, he will always make certain that he drives the best car that he can afford; status symbols are particularly important to the Hero man.

The Hero Parent

Home life means a great deal to the Hero, and family roots run deep. Heroes are one of the most caring signs when it comes to the well-being of their children, although emotionally they may be somewhat restrained. They will encourage their young in their school work, but may be unresponsive to their personal problems. Typically Heroes feel that others will be as strong as they, and tend to lack sympathy with those in emotional crises. 'Just forget about it,' might be an easy solution for the Hero, but others are not so strong. However, Heroes always make certain that their children are well-dressed, fed and cared for, no matter what personal sacrifices are necessary.

The Hero Child

From a very early age the Hero child will be a responsive and eager learner. Hero children are inquisitive in the extreme, wanting to know the reason – the full reason – for everything. They are seldom put off with a half-answer. They work diligently at school and usually do well in class. There are seldom bad reports of the Hero child. They are keen to succeed in sports and many become school captains.

Heroes prefer routine and dislike environmental change. A new school or move of home can considerably upset the young Hero. Providing that their surroundings remain consistent, the Hero child is usually easy to please.

The Hero has a constructive attitude to life, and few Hero children will deliberately cause trouble or break their toys. They are particularly polite to adults, but there is a tendency for the Hero child to be overbearing with other children. They are seldom bullies, although they usually insist on taking the lead with their friends.

The Hero Friend

Heroes are peace-loving and amiable, wishing to live in harmony with their associates and neighbours. Few Heroes are responsible for causing trouble of any kind. When annoyed, however, they have quite a temper. Beware of trying the patience of the Hero. Once hurt or angered, the Hero is slow to forgive and will never forget. They make loyal and supportive friends, but bad enemies.

Both male and female Heroes are possessive in relationships and friendships alike. They choose their acquaintances carefully, making sure they mix with others who share their beliefs and sentiments. Accordingly, there are seldom conflicts of interest. However, if one of their friends should change their attitudes or find others with whom to associate, the Hero may feel personally insulted. Heroes make devoted friends but are uneasy about casual acquaintances of any kind.

The Hero Partner

Both Hero men and women are passionate and uninhibited lovers, although romantic sentiment is not a natural Hero trait. Keen to establish order and routine in their lives, they tend to marry young. This can sometimes lead to hasty decisions. In fact, marriage is about the only time in the Hero's life when they do not think long and hard about a commitment. If the right partner is found, the Hero will do everything to ensure that the marriage succeeds.

The Hero enjoys flattery and admiration, particularly from the opposite sex. This sometimes results in wrong impressions. The fact that both Hero men and women are inclined to innocent flirtation can lead their partners to believe that they are being unfaithful. This is seldom true of the Hero. They are usually the most loyal partners of any sign.

Those born in this cycle are especially hurt when a relationship fails. Break-ups demoralize the Hero considerably, and their entire life may suffer as a result. When a relationship ends the Hero sees it as a personal failure. Heroes have considerable difficulty coping with turmoil or coming to terms with change.

Affinity Signs

The Dragon: The industrious and optimistic Dragon is admired by the Hero. Both signs share the ability to consistently devote themselves to a single goal or objective.

The Sphinx: The Sphinx is the sign which the Hero admires the most. Their ability to make something out of nothing, together with their keen financial instinct, are greatly respected by the Hero.

The Serpent: The Serpent is a sign of wisdom and those

born in this cycle are particularly creative in practical endeavours. The Hero is a materialist and so the two signs compliment one another. Both signs lead similar social lives and close friendships and attachments are common.

The Genie: Heroes often find themselves attracted to a Genie of the opposite sex. The Genie is particularly vulnerable to the self-assured Hero, while the Hero enjoys the flattery and attention they receive from Genii.

Problem Signs

The Swallow: The Swallow is far too sensitive and emotional for the Hero, while the Hero is too overbearing for the Swallow. The two signs have little in common, and their outlooks on life differ considerably.

The Oryx and the Phoenix: The Hero likes consistency. Both these signs are too erratic by far.

Assari: The Assari hates being controlled, while Heroes love being in control.

Other Signs

Cascaya: These signs often have many interests in common. However, Cascayans hate to be told what to do. The Hero is sometimes too authoritative for the Cascayan liking.

Etana: The Etana is a particularly affectionate sign, and the Hero tends to distrust open displays of affection. The Hero, however, can sometimes provide an emotional balance for the Etana.

The Griffin: Griffins and Heroes mix well socially as

both are polite and confident signs. When working together, however, there can be clashes of interest. In marriage there may be problems as both signs are exceptionally stubborn.

The Hero: Heroes get on great with Heroes of the opposite sex. They both love order and consistency in a relationship. Heroes of the same sex, however, tend to clash.

The Huntress: The Hero admires the resourceful Huntress, but the Huntress often finds the Hero far too conventional in approach to life.

Famous Heroes
Grace Jones. Born: 19 May 1952.

Typically Hero, Grace Jones is fiercely independent. With strong will and determination she is one of life's winners. Grace is a natural leader and like most Heroes she does not suffer fools lightly. Like many born in this sign, Grace is outspoken and may find it difficult to control her temper. Any burst of negative emotion, however, is usually the result of provocation. As with most Heroes, Grace generally directs her energy toward a desired objective. Grace's flamboyant personality commands attention, often respect, although some may find her overbearing. However, love or hate her, like most who are born in this cycle Grace is impossible to ignore.

Marilyn Monroe. Born: 1 June 1926.

A very different kind of Hero is Marilyn Monroe. Although few would immediately think of her as having typical Hero traits, she did take the world by storm. Indeed, she has become a genuine folk heroine for millions around the world. It was not simply Marilyn's figure or stunning looks that made her the most sought-after woman in the world, but the powerful Hero attributes of presence and irresistible personality. Like many Hero women, she had a natural and earthy modesty, and often found media attention disturbing and difficult to handle. Privacy is something which the Hero greatly treasures and, sadly for Marilyn, this was something she seldom enjoyed.

Bob Dylan. Born: 24 May 1941.

Artistic Heroes usually have a down-to-earth approach to creativity and Bob Dylan is typical in this respect. His unique ability to put poetry to music made him the king of popular ballad. Although few Heroes pursue a musical career, those who do make certain that there is a very practical purpose to their work. Bob Dylan is not only a superstar musician, he is a singer whose name became synonymous with the protest songs of the 1960s. Like most Heroes, Bob Dylan is not afraid to say what he feels and express what he believes.

Fate and Fortune

Over the course of the year Heroes can expect the following influences to affect their lives during the separate lunar cycles:

Cascaya: This may be a time of considerable frustration for the Hero. Cascaya is a sign of intangibility and the Hero dislikes anything that cannot be pinned down. In the Cascaya month Heroes may find it particularly difficult to get to grips with the circumstances surrounding them.

The Phoenix: Many Heroes find the renewing Phoenix brings them fresh opportunities, particularly of a financial or business nature. Affairs of the heart may be problematic, however, due to a tendency by Heroes to apply themselves too much to material matters.

The Hero: Heroes should be careful during their own month. They should give and take a little more, and accept that not everything is going to plan. Others have their own ideas which the Hero should take into consideration. If the Hero takes things as they come, this can be an extremely favourable month for romance.

Assari: Heroes are generally down-to-earth in their approach to most matters. Assari is a particularly imaginative sign, so ideas that the Hero may previously have considered impractical may be discovered to be quite feasible after all.

The Genie: The Genie month is the Hero's most favourable period for romance and adventure. Although the Hero seldom lets themselves be carried away by emotion, they may have little choice during this particular cycle. Any Hero looking for a new love in their life may be pleasantly surprised during this month.

The Griffin: This is a time of financial reward for many Heroes. Good news, especially concerning monetary matters, is to be expected. The Hero is not a gambler by nature, but a risk taken during this cycle is likely to be rewarded.

The Oryx: The Oryx is a sign of movement, change and versatility. The Hero is sometimes loath to change direction. During this month, however, they may be impelled to rethink a strategy. Whether a business or domestic affair, a decision requiring a new approach needs attention. The Hero should beware of expecting everything to remain the same. Any Hero considering a change of work or location may find it profitable to start searching at this time.

Etana: During the month of Etana the Hero should make time for relaxation. Sport and other leisure activities are favourably placed, and vacations taken during the cycle of Etana can be especially fulfilling for the Hero.

The Serpent: The wise Serpent brings contemplation to the Hero. At this time of year the Hero may become somewhat withdrawn in social circumstances. Relationships, particularly with colleagues or close friends, may suffer.

The Dragon: Domestic matters may require much of the Hero's attention. Heroes should try to divide their time equally between work, rest and play. Unusual occurrences around the end of the month may bring a radical change in everyday affairs. This is often a favourable month for love, romance and affairs of the heart.

The Sphinx: The Sphinx month is often a time of conundrum, and complex circumstances are likely to confront the Hero. Friends, relatives or work colleagues will be particularly helpful and may even provide solutions to longstanding problems the Hero has been unable to resolve. The Sphinx acts as the messenger bearer for the Hero. Surprising news can be expected around the end of the month.

The Swallow: The high-flying Swallow and the earthy Hero are signs often worlds apart. This may be a time of little change in the Hero's life.

The Huntress: It is often during a Huntress month that the Hero will act completely out of character. Based simply on intuition or instinct, the Hero may make an inspired decision. A new enterprise or relationship forged during this cycle is likely to bring considerable reward for the Hero.

ASSARI

Approximate Calendar Month
JUNE

Sign Chart Letter
D

ASSARI

LIKE the winged ibex Assari, this is a sign of grace and charm. Although the winged ibex is elegant in flight, however, those born in this cycle are not naturally at home in the air. Usually possessing great artistic flair, they do not accept art for its own sake, seeking instead practical applications for their creations. Assaris may get carried away with enthusiasm, but work best if they control and direct their creativity. Like the winged ibex of lengend, once aloft they fly with the grace of a swallow. Unfortunately, they find difficulty taking off; a lack of confidence or direction may be the cause of many problems. Once they discover a balance between the down-to-earth and the imaginative, those born in this sign are free to accomplish outstanding achievements. Their true vocation realized, nothing can stop the Assari. Although not the epitome of patience, the Assari has an abundance of creative energy and can soar to remarkable heights.

Many Assaris have both spiritual and material aspirations. It is as though they have a foot in two worlds. Although the realms of imagination are sought by the Assari, most are realists and few are content to live in a world of make-believe. Their intuitive decisions are often implemented with firm, rational logic. Assaris are social creatures, and a combination of fun and hard work can easily be enjoyed by those born in this sign.

Assari is an unusual sign and shares much in common with the Swallow. If circumstances are in their favour Assaris can be outgoing and extrovert. Yet, if they do not have the right support or encouragement they are prone to shyness and withdrawal. Somewhat surprisingly, they enjoy being the centre of attention; even the shy Assari will indirectly compensate. Many famous artists and novelists are Assaris. Even though they may spend much of their time in seclusion, their work ensures their fame.

Positive Characteristics

Having natural charm, the Assari is both expressive and theatrical. With easily stimulated emotions, they have tremendous enthusiasm for new ideas. They share an originality of thinking with a quick intellect and good memory. Assaris have the capacity to learn easily. They have a romantic temperament coupled with great love of travel and adventure. Neat and tidy, Assaris take pride in their personal appearance.

Negative Characteristics

Impatience and intolerance often result in considerable frustration, and difficulties arise mainly through restlessness. For those born in this cycle there is a tendency to fly to extremes and irritability can strain relationships. Assaris have strong likes and dislikes and their emotions are easily roused. They are often impulsive by nature and extravagance is often a problem. Envy is sometimes an Assari trait, and jealousy needs to be controlled.

Appearance

The typical Assari has gentle features, with large, sometimes sorrowful eyes. Although alert and active, few Assaris are fidgets or rapid, erratic movers. Most are graceful in their movements. Assari women have a sensual appeal, while Assari men tend to be smooth and sophisticated. The facial features of both are particularly expressive. When annoyed, the Assari will open their eyes wide with surprise, then frown disapprovingly.

Health

Strangely, many Assaris have problems with their feet and breaking in new shoes can be agony. They are particularly vulnerable to colds and flu, after which many suffer from lingering coughs. Bronchitis and other chest complaints are common for Assaris who are smokers. On the positive side, few Assaris suffer from digestive complaints; ulcers are rare for those born in this sign.

The Formula for Success

The strongest motivating urge in the average Assari is to enjoy life to the full. They have the enviable knack of living well, even if they have little money. Those born in this sign are experts at obtaining the best from most situations. Many Assaris are fortunate in monetary matters, through sound intuition regarding investments. Indeed, many of the world's most successful gamblers and investors in the stock-market are born in this sign. Assaris have a generous nature and gain much contentment by helping others. If those close to Assaris are happy, so are they.

Words of Advice

Assaris find it difficult to run their lives on simple, well-organized lines. They often find themselves in difficult predicaments, usually due to good intentions and a tendency to expect others to act as considerately as they. Although generous, the Assari has a self-indulgent streak. If life is not full of variety and stimulation they soon become bored. They may forget their obligations and migrate to new endeavours. Assaris also lack will-power, needing the moral support of others to achieve success. They are especially sensitive to adverse opinion and may admit defeat simply because someone else has told them that something will fail. Although they are strongly individualistic, they are usually anything but loners. To fly high, Assaris constantly need the encouragement of friends and associates – they are prone to stagnation and misery if left without support.

Suitable Occupations.

Intuition, imagination and versatility are Assari qualities, and many born in this sign achieve the best results once they have discovered an application for these traits. Ideal occupations for Assaris are those offering scope for their artistic talents. The Assari is one of the most imaginative signs and many excel in all branches of the arts. Dancing, singing, acting and drama have strong appeal. The more retiring Assaris may concentrate on painting, writing or sculpture, which allows them to be apart from others for much of their time. Their much-needed appreciation comes via the appeal of their work.

Most Assaris commit themselves to the well-being of others, so social work and health care have strong appeal. Many Assari women make excellent child minders or carers for the sick or elderly. Assari men are often found involved in youth schemes and other forms of community work.

Assaris make popular employers, supervisors and managers. Unlike some signs whom power or influence may corrupt, few Assaris will adopt a superior attitude when dealing with subordinates.

The Assari at Work

The Assari can be most misleading. A shy Assari will be strong and motivated in times of crisis, whereas the tougher Assari may be a real softie inside. Work colleagues are often surprised by the Assari who suddenly displays abilities or talents they least expected. It is a mistake for any prospective employer to readily categorize the Assari, especially during an interview. What you see is not all you get with the self-conscious Assari.

Assaris may not handle their own affairs with the thrift of some signs, but when it comes to business matters they have a good head for profit. A shrewd financial instinct often makes them accurate in their appraisal of market trends. Whether a shop-floor worker or a business manager, the Assari usually knows precisely how an enterprise is likely to fare. As employees, Assaris work well in teams, although they are not at their best in front-line sales. They are too easily distracted by adverse criticism of themselves or their product.

The Assari Woman

The Assari woman is a great conversationalist and an eager listener – her company is much appreciated by men. Even the shy Assari has an entertaining countenance when apart from the crowd – she too, enjoys much attention. Many women envy her popularity and accordingly she may experience some difficulty in making close female friends.

The Assari woman is neat and tidy, although she is far more concerned with her personal appearance than with the state of her home. She usually spends so much time concentrating on her hair, clothes and make-up, that housework is often left unattended. It can come as a complete shock for a first-time visitor to an Assari woman's home – her personal living space is nowhere near as orderly as expected.

Assari women prefer particularly feminine fashions, and few will be caught out in jeans or dull, efficient suits. Pinks, yellows and pastel shades are often her choice of colours, while jewellery is small, delicate and tasteful.

Many Assari women who continue in work after starting a family will do so in a self-employed capacity. They are particularly astute regarding style and fashion, and many beauty consultants are Assari mothers in part-time work.

The Assari Man

Assari men are cool, calm and collected, and usually the centre of attention. Like his female counterpart, he is popular with the opposite sex, and others may be jealous of the attention he receives. He is not a fast-fire talker, however, and his sense of humour leaves something to be desired. Instead, he has a smooth-talking charm that usually appeals to women rather than men. Few Assari men are boisterous or vulgar in mixed company, and their refinement may exclude them from many 'macho' activities.

The Assari man may play an active role in sport and leisure pursuits, but he works best in a leadership or organizing capacity rather than as 'one of the boys'. Many Assari men have an interest in politics, and the trades union movement includes a considerable number of Assaris amongst its higher ranks. All political parties benefit from the contributions of Assari members and the keenness of their support. Most conservationist and charity organizations also have a large number of Assaris playing important roles.

With his partner, the Assari man will be gallant and accommodating, if not a little old-fashioned. He will treat his lover like a lady, and cannot resist buying her chocolates and flowers. In today's world many women regard such behaviour as condescending, and may even consider the Assari a chauvinist. Others who adore being pampered may discover that a date with the Assari man can be a romantic dream.

The Assari Parent

Many Assaris enjoy strong family ties. The more people to love and be loved by, the happier they are. In many ways Assari parents may be a little too lax with their children. They strongly disapprove of punishment of any kind, preferring instead to reward their children for success rather than scold them for failure. Assaris are one of the best signs for comforting a child who has failed an examination, is experiencing difficulty at school, or is in distress of any kind. Many Assaris spoil their children rotten. They so love to see them happy that they may sometimes ignore the need for firmer control. Some children may take advantage of the Assari and turn on the tears whenever there is something they want. Assaris make wonderfully devoted parents but not the best of teachers. A class-full of boisterous youngsters will soon learn to walk all over the accommodating Assari.

The Assari Child

So often a gentle, loving child, the sensitive Assari needs much encouragement to face the harsher realities of life. The romantic painting of the tearful, wide-eyed orphan, so popular in Victorian times, often epitomizes the Assari child. They are dreamers, and many have invisible childhood friends. Even those that do not will regularly talk to themselves and can spend hours playing alone.

Assari children mature later than those of other signs. Sometimes this means that they are bullied or badgered by older children. In their teens, however, they quickly learn to stand up for themselves. Assaris are not aggressive by nature, and many abhor physical violence. When absolutely necessary, however, they are quite prepared to meet like with like.

Assari children are especially creative and many excel in the arts. The sciences, however, seldom appeal to the Assari child. Teachers may complain about their performance in subjects like mathematics, chemistry or physics. Few children born in this sign pay much attention to lessons in which they have absolutely no interest.

The Assari Friend

There is a mercurial quality about the Assari which often confuses friends. Unconsciously, Assaris can adopt the attitudes, habits and mannerisms of those with whom they are closely associated. This is one reason that Assaris are so popular with the opposite sex – they can be all things to all people.

Although Assaris enjoy flattery and attention with respect to their appearance, most retain a genuine modesty regarding their work. Indeed, some find it embarrassing when they are praised for their professional achievements. Again, this can be confusing to

Assari friends, who may wonder if they have somehow offended with a heart-felt compliment. Assari modesty is genuine, although some of their reactions are not. They are natural actors, not above feigning enthusiasm for something in which they have no real interest. The Assari may seem riveted by your conversation, despite actually being bored stiff. Assaris are especially polite and hate to offend. They have, however, no intention of going through the same experience twice. So often casual acquaintances are bewildered when the Assari makes an excuse not to join them for a drink. Didn't they have a great time last week? Assari associates should make doubly certain that the Assari is truly happy.

The Assari Partner

The personal life of the Assari would provide rich material for the romantic novelist. Falling in and out of love is a regular habit for those born in this sign. Assaris share an idealistic, if not unrealistic, attitude to romance. Even if a relationship ends in disaster, they remain eternally optimistic about future affairs. They seem to believe that love is exactly as it is in the movies. If a relationship fails to blossom they are often deeply hurt, and usually blame themselves. Assaris, however, are not possessive lovers and few will continue to throw unwanted attentions in an ex-partner's direction.

Assaris enjoy romance to the extent that marital commitments seldom come early. When they eventually do settle down, Assari's husbands are expected to pull their weight with the housework, while Assari's wives are usually left to handle all domestic affairs. Assari women, in particular, seem to get their partner to do exactly what they want – at precisely the right moment they can turn on the tears or charm.

Though vulnerable to passing infatuation, the Assari is capable of considerable loyalty. If love begins to fade, however, Assari fidelity will soon follow suit. The Assari hates to hurt another's feelings, and sometimes they find it difficult to terminate one affair before another begins.

Affinity Signs

The Oryx: The Assari particularly enjoys the company of the Oryx. The Assari's romanticism is often inspired by the Oryx's adventurous spirit.

The Phoenix: The Assari similarly likes the company of the Phoenix. Both have a romantic temperament and can inspire one another to great success.

The Griffin: The Griffin and the Assari are particularly compatible signs, especially concerning romantic affiliations. Both share common interests, whilst their personalities are sufficiently different not to clash.

The Huntress: Assaris are often attracted to the unconventional Huntress, while Huntresses move towards those with imagination. These signs are most compatible, and many successful marriages and business partnerships result.

Problem Signs

The Hero: The Assari hates being controlled, while Heroes love being in control.

Assari: The Assari is not a sign who finds it easy to mix well with others similar to themselves. Two Assaris may find that they are constantly in competition with one another.

Cascaya: The Assari is too sentimental for Cascaya. The Assari seeks close relationships and has a need for firm, emotional commitments. The Cascaya feels too restricted by such demands.

Other Signs

The Genie: In many ways the Genie shares a romantic and imaginative disposition with the Assari. The two signs may find that they clash if both try to gain the attention of the same person or group. As partners, however, they compliment one another, sharing many similar interests.

Etana: Etanas and Assaris both allow their imaginations a free reign. Consequently, the two signs may behave somewhat irresponsibly when together.

The Serpent: The Assari finds the learned Serpent of considerable interest. They may, however, distrust the Serpent's reposeful, laid-back approach to life.

The Dragon: Relationships between Assaris and Dragons are particularly volatile. They may adore one another, sharing a love of adventure, travel and excitement. When together, however, both may find their emotions too readily stimulated and arguments can follow. These signs often have a love-hate relationship.

The Sphinx: Assaris generally admire the clever Sphinx, whereas Sphinxes often find the romantic Assari a stimulating companion.

The Swallow: Swallows and Assaris both share an interest in the exotic and unusual aspects of life. Close friendships and relationships are possible, although marriages between these two signs may sometimes suffer due to a lack of practical considerations.

Famous Assaris

Princess Diana. Born: 1 July 1961.

Typically Assari, Princess Diana took time to adapt to her sudden exposure to public attention. She is naturally shy, lacking initial confidence in her own abilities. However, like the winged ibex, which when airborne flew with the grace of a swallow, Diana, once accustomed to the international limelight, took elegantly to her new role. Assaris often find it hard to change, but they learn quickly and lend their own particular style to whatever they do. The unique grace and charm of the Assari is displayed by Diana, having become one of the world's most popular women.

Clint Eastwood. Born: 31 May 1930.

Unlike some who have been elevated to stardom, Clint Eastwood has retained a genuine modesty concerning his achievements. Many born in the Assari sign share a diffidence about their success, indeed finding it embarrassing when they are praised or flattered. Like many Assari men, Clint is the epitome of the cool, calm and collected male, often hiding a certain lack of self-confidence. The Assari is a sign of accomplishments in both artistic and practical affairs. Clint has incorporated these Assari traits in his work as an actor, a director and as a politician.

John F. Kennedy. Born: 29 May 1917.

The versatility of the Assari is amply demonstrated by

President John F. Kennedy. He utilized an arsenal of varying traits and attributes in the pursuit of his career. An accomplished politician and administrator, he was also one of the greatest orators of his era. Typically Assari, President Kennedy continued with the daunting task of government while retaining a fresh and lively disposition. Although in a position of supreme responsibility, President Kennedy always displayed the Assari warm and affectionate manner. Unlike some who may change once they achieve power, the Assari usually remains unaltered by success. Once they have accomplished a goal, those born in this sign can complete their schedule, no matter how difficult, in a natural and unassuming way.

Fate and Fortune

Over the course of the year Assaris can expect the following influences to affect their lives during the separate lunar cycles:

Cascaya: The spray of the waterfall is held as mist in the air. The airy Assari will often find that they are relied on by others to support them during this month. Most Assaris like attention and are helpful by nature. However, they may find that they are restricted by the constant demands of others.

The Phoenix: In legend the Phoenix continually rose from the ashes. The Phoenix month is a time for new opportunities for the Assari. Something long-awaited may come to fruition. New friendships or relationships are possible. Sport and leisure activities, even games of chance, are favourable for the Assari at this time.

The Hero: The Hero is a sign of authority. Many Assaris distrust authority and especially hate being ordered around. This is a month where the Assari may find greatest difficulty. Someone close to the Assari could attempt to persuade them to act against their wishes. The Assari should stand firm, and avoid becoming entangled in arguments and quarrels.

Assari: During the month of their own sign Assaris are in their imaginative element. New ideas are forever occurring to them and fresh possibilities are eagerly grasped. This is a particularly favourable time for anything to do with music or the arts.

The Genie: The imaginative and adventurous Assari is well-placed for romance during the month of the Genie. An existing partnership is likely to be enhanced by new prospects, particularly concerning domestic matters and the home. An Assari on the lookout for a new partner may be pleasantly surprised. New acquaintances and friendships are possible.

The Griffin: The Griffin and the Assari are particularly compatible signs. The Griffin is a positive influence for bringing imaginative ideas to practical fruition. Dreams can literally come true for the Assari in this month. For the Assari with any inclination to change work or location, now is a good time to start looking for a new home or occupation.

The Oryx: The horned Oryx and the horned Assari have much in common. This month can be a time of success, especially in business matters. However, Assaris should avoid interlocking horns with the influences of this month. They should let things be as they are, rather than how they would wish them to be.

Etana: Etana flew high on the back of an eagle. Both

signs of flight, Etana and Assari merge to bring positive influences for escapism. This is the best time of year for an Assari to take a vacation. Weekends away can be particularly romantic. A favourable time for love generally. Business matters or difficult decisions concerning domestic life are best left until Assaris have their feet more firmly on the ground.

The Serpent: The Serpent acts as a message bearer for the Assari. News received during the early days of this month can result in a new outlook on life for the Assari. This is also a time well-placed for financial and monetary matters.

The Dragon: At no other time of the year is the Assari more likely to lose patience than during the month of the fiery Dragon. Problems in relationships or with close friends or colleagues may occur as a result of Assari irritability.

The Sphinx: For the Assari this month is a time of learning. Those Assaris involved in academic pursuits will find this a particularly fruitful time of the year. In general, Assaris will find that solutions to problems will present themselves. Others should respect the Assari's point of view during the month of the Sphinx – it is often wise, inspired and deeply intuitive.

The Swallow: If there is a lurking problem in the Assari's life, this is the time of year when it is most likely to erupt. If there are difficulties in relationships, with friends or at work, they are likely to hit a crisis point. If something should end or change, this may be the time to act.

The Huntress: The Huntress month is especially linked

to financial matters as far as the Assari is concerned. An unexpected windfall is possible. Any new enterprise intiated now is likely to reap rewards.

THE GENIE

Approximate Calendar Month
JULY

Sign Chart Letter
E

THE GENIE

IN Babylonian mythology genii were benevolent and helpful spirits. Acting as intermediaries between heaven and earth, they were thought to influence dreams, inspiration and imagination. Like their mythical counterparts, those born in this cycle are creative, intuitive and imaginative. Natural actors and charmers, they are never more in their element than when they are in the public eye. Often dreamers, the intentions of the Genie are sometimes hard to fathom. The genie of legend could inspire a man or woman with foresight, they had the power to influence the future and bring magic and mystery into the world. Mystical subjects often have a strong appeal to those born in this sign, and there is a marked tendency for Genii to hold unusual or revolutionary ideas. With both an alluring personality and a love of adventure, the Genie is a born romantic.

Genii share a love of variety and adventure although, unlike some signs, they are not so intrepid as to endanger themselves or others in their pursuits. Genii may be spirited but they need their comforts and security too much to risk them in all-or-nothing endeavours. The genie of legend journeyed from the gods to humanity; a typical trait of this sign is a strong desire to travel. Genii, however, need a secure environment to return to. Few Genii are eager to uproot themselves from the place they call home.

Genii are generally kind and helpful. However, they have strong likes and dislikes and have little time for those with whom they have no affinity. No one should have much difficulty determining whether they happen to be in the Genie's good or bad books.

Positive Characteristics

For the Genie, high ideals and ambitions go hand-in-hand with a lively intelligence. There is a love of travel and adventure and artistic pursuits have a strong attraction. Often popular, the Genie's carefree enthusiasm can bring out the best in others. Many born in this sign have talents connected with the performing arts. They have keen powers of observation and are quick to grasp the essence of most situations. With an appealing imagination and an intense appreciation of beauty, many Genii share an interest in environmental issues.

Negative Characteristics

Genii have difficulty in concentrating, especially when they have too much on their minds. Few find it easy to handle more than one problem at a time. A failure to apply themselves to intricate endeavours may reduce their chances of success. Worry and indecision also act to hold back progress for many born in this sign. Genii hate to feel they are being manipulated, and often a resentment of authority can complicate relationships in business or at work. Many Genii are dreamers and share unrealistic expectations concerning their endeavours. Genii do not recover easily from failure; stagnation may result from an unsuccessful enterprise.

Appearance

The Genie is a sign of elegance. The woman of this cycle seems almost to float or glide as she walks. The Genie man will have a purposeful and determined gait; he is far more graceful in his movements than men of many other signs. Most Genie activity is conducted with deliberate and mindful composure. They refuse to sprawl or slouch even when relaxed. Genii are almost feline in their poise. Like the sleeping cat, they will seem as refined at rest as when fully alert. When they stir, they even stretch like a cat. Few born in this sign will be scruffy or unkempt in any circumstance. They do, however, share a lazy attitude concerning laborious domestic chores. Most Genii will rely on others to tidy up after them.

Health

The Genie is one of the healthiest of signs. Few born in this cycle will suffer from repeated bouts of colds or flu. Indeed, after childhood, viral infections of any kind are rare for Genii. Allergies are the most common complaints of this group. The Genie's highly-active immune system can often result in such problems as asthma or hay-fever. Many Genii suffer skin rashes, often as the consequence of nervous tension. Worry may result in headaches or nausea, particularly if the Genie is in distress.

The Formula for Success

To their loved ones and relations the Genie is both generous and kind. To their enemies they make formidable opponents, especially if someone has done something to upset their friends. They are particularly receptive to the problems of those close to them; always ready to listen, they provide a firm shoulder on which to cry.

The Genie is highly ambitious, although they may need the support and direction of others to fulfil their dreams. This is seldom a problem, however, as the Genie is one of the most influential of signs. They have the marvellous ability to manipulate the attitudes and decisions of others. Those born in this cycle possess extraordinary intuition, enabling them to predict or determine the actions and intentions of those about them. In many walks of life the Genie's hunches and insights will often prove uncannily accurate.

Words of Advice

Genies are expressive but have difficulty expressing heart-felt emotions. If their love and affection is not reciprocated they may become withdrawn and depressed. They do not respond well to rejection, whether in business, friendship or love. The Genie is also inconsistent in temperament and is inclined to be silent or moody at times. Those born in this sign are strongly advised not to expect too much from others, or from what may seem a promising enterprise.

The Genie is also one of the worst signs for time-keeping. They always leave things to the last possible moment. Coupled with the fact that they need plenty of time to preen themselves and prepare for any occasion, this means that the Genie is nearly always late. Imaginative temperament results in an absent-minded Genie. Moreover, they have a tendency to daydream. If they are engaged in something which fails to fully absorb their attention, Genii are apt to lapse into a state of reverie. Most of all, Genii are forgetful and forever mislaying their possessions. The Genie should learn to concentrate. More especially, they should avoid the compulsion to put off until later what can easily be done right away.

Suitable Occupations

The Genie is a paradoxical sign as far as work is concerned. They have lofty and far-reaching ambition but need the constant support and encouragement of others. A lack of self-motivation may lead Genii to drift into occupations they cannot abide. Ideally, however, anything connnected with entertainment is the perfect career for the Genie. Drama has strong appeal, as does singing and music. The Genie has excellent coordination and many Genii make superb dancers.

Careers in the travel or leisure industry are also appealing to Genii. They have a flair for the dramatic in any situation, and many positions in public relations are successfully occupied by Genii.

The Genie at Work

The Genie has strong likes and dislikes. Few born in this sign will spare much time for those they cannot abide. This may lead to complications in working relationships. The Genie finds it hard and tiresome to exchange niceties, or feign affinity, with colleagues or business acquaintances they dislike. Often their honest and forthright manner can prejudice success or advancement in their careers.

The Genie boss may be an enthusiastic and dedicated employer, but is inclined to favour some employees over others. This can often be detrimental to the smooth-running of a business, and resignations are common when an enterprise appoints a new Genie manager. However, before long, the Genie will gather around them the team with whom they are happiest to work. They make few pretensions with opponents. Most people who fall on the wrong side of a Genie are unlikely to remain in close proximity for long.

The Genie Woman

The especially feminine Genie is popular with men. Many Genie women share a timeless aura of youth. There is something of the little girl in the Genie woman throughout her life; few outgrow the desire for fun, frolics and frivolity. Consequently, she is not the most eager of signs to settle down and raise a family. She enjoys love, adventure and romance far too much to throw it all away at the first available opportunity. When she does choose a partner with whom to share her life, she will do so only after much deliberation.

Born in a sign of elegance, the female of this cycle takes great pride in her personal appearance. She spares little expense on her cosmetics and jewellery; few Genie women will be caught dead wearing cheap perfume or fake stones. She has no particular preference for colours and will dress to suit her mood. The Genie is a woman of considerable style.

Provided she has a partner who can afford to keep her in the manner she expects, the Genie woman will have no hesitation abandoning her career. Many women of this sign will go for men who are prepared to let them remain the belle of the ball for the rest of their lives. Woe betide the man who tries to prevent her from continuing to look her best after marriage. She expects and needs love and affection – but nothing is more likely to dampen the Genie's feelings than a possessive and jealous partner.

The Genie Man

The Genie man is often laid-back in his socializing. He may be open and friendly, but he prefers to keep his cool. He is as concerned about his appearance as his female counterpart although, for him, it is more a matter of physique. He is often an avid body-builder; if not, he will certainly devote much time and effort to recreational activities which keep him in shape. He is especially fond of sport. Even if he is not personally involved in competition, he will follow his favourite team or event with zeal. The Genie man is an ardent supporter and a keen spectator.

Although generally good-humoured, the Genie is not beyond resorting to physical conflict if necessary. Like the female of this sign, he has quite a temper if pushed too far. By contrast, he may be somewhat shy in the company of women. However, he can be the epitome of the smooth-talking charmer once the ice has been broken. The Genie man is not over-keen on parties and organized social events, preferring more spontaneous enjoyment. He loves to surprise the woman in his life with an impromptu dinner or a weekend away in the country. Indeed, if he lives in the city he will need to get away to the country from time to time, simply to relax. The Genie man is somewhat possessive by nature and dislikes having to share his lady's company with anyone else.

The Genie loves a challenge, providing it does not disrupt his life-style. Like his female counterpart, the Genie man is eager for adventure. He has a lively sense of humour and intends to enjoy every moment to the full. Most Genii are popular and fun-loving. However, beyond the contented veneer of the Genie man, lies a powerful drive to succeed and a spirit of pure determination.

The Genie Parent

Most Genies share the need to live in a clean, uncluttered environment. Unfortunately, they just hate the mundane work involved in keeping their homes neat and tidy. The desire for order will usually outweigh their lazy streak; housework and other domestic chores will eventually get done. Once they have undertaken the considerable effort necessary to complete these laborious tasks, they will not take kindly to someone coming along and messing them up. A prime trait of the Genie parent is to go to great lengths to keep their children from being dirty or untidy. They allot specific rooms as play-rooms, ruling other parts of the house strictly out of bounds. They can be fairly strict with their children regarding personal appearance, although in other matters Genii are some of the most lenient of parents. They are liberal in outlook, seldom expecting their offspring to share their views. Few Genii try to force an unwanted career upon their children. Their advice: 'Be whatever you like, so long as you're a good one'.

The Genie Child

Genie children have strong attachments and share a deep bond with their parents. Provided they are reared in a happy home, few born in this sign will be eager to leave. The Genie child is ultra-sensitive to the family atmosphere, quick to respond to the moods of parents, brothers or sisters. It is especially important that their environment should be calm and happy. Genie children are especially susceptible to the negative influence of parental quarrels, even well into adolescence.

The Genie is an honest and loving child, although many lack the confidence of other signs. They need much support from parents and teachers alike if they are to make the best of opportunities. It is usually later in life before the Genie will learn the ways and wiles of the big wide world.

The Genie Friend

The Genie is a sociable sign, although most born in this cycle refuse to indulge in idle gossip. Accordingly, they make trustworthy friends. Acquaintances can rest assured that their secrets are safe with the Genie. Something told in confidence to a Genie of either sex will seldom be broadcast further. Indeed, this is the least nosey of any sign. For the Genie, other people's business is their own private affair.

Due to their fine intuition there is a mysterious, ethereal quality to the Genie. So often they seem to know exactly what someone is thinking, or take the relevant action at precisely the right time. A word of advice for the Genie's friends and employers: listen well and consider carefully any idea the Genie proposes. Their insights are frequently well-founded and their hunches are often remarkably accurate. They are, however, inclined to change their plans at the very last moment.

Although a romantic, the Genie is not the best of signs for remembering birthdays, anniversaries and special occasions. If the Genie has forgotten an important engagement, friends should avoid taking offence or thinking that this is in any way a personal rebuff. Genii can even forget their *own* birthdays.

The Genie Partner

Although at home in the limelight, Genii do need their own space and privacy. This is particularly true for their privacy of mind. One thing that Genii cannot stand is someone asking them what they are thinking. If the Genie seems remote or lost in a world of thought, do not be tempted to ask: 'What's on your mind?' You are likely to be told to mind your own business. Time to think alone is an important requirement in the life of any Genie. Genie partners should also remember this: the Genie may love you dearly, but encroachment on their personal space is strictly forbidden.

In love and marriage the Genie is far less impulsive than many signs. Even when they are attracted to someone immediately, it will be some time before they are prepared to make any kind of firm commitments. If their courting is not allowed to proceed slowly, stage by careful stage, then the whole relationship may be annulled. Rush the Genie and you may risk everything. Indeed, Genii hate to be hurried at anything in their lives. In married life the Genie will also expect to retain his or her own set of interests. Few Genii are prepared to abandon their former lives for the sake of a jealous partner.

Genii of both sexes expect a romance to be romantic, with everything that entails. The Genie woman adores being treated like a lady, and Genie man loves to wine and dine a girl in style.

Affinity Signs

The Oryx: The Oryx particularly likes the company of the Genie. The Genie's romanticism makes them an eager audience for the imaginative ideas of the Oryx. Genii often need others to continually inspire them. The accommodating and enthusiastic Oryx is ideal in this respect.

The Hero: Heroes often find themselves attracted to Genies of the opposite sex. The Genie is particularly drawn to the self-assurance of the Hero, while the Hero enjoys the flattery and attention they in turn receive from the Genie.

The Griffin: Although Genii are romantic and fun-loving, they desperately need security. Griffins are not averse to romanticism, they simply need inspiration. These two signs compliment one another nicely.

The Phoenix: Phoenixes love being in the company of Genii and vice versa. Both signs have a romantic attitude to life.

Etana: The Etana is often admired by the Genie for their originality and courageous attitude. Strong attachments are possible and relationships are often successful. The Etana can bring many interesting possibilities into the Genie's life, whereas the Genie's more down-to-eath approach, particularly to financial matters, can restrain the impulsive Etana.

Problem Signs

The Genie: Genii often need the encouragement or ideas of others to start them moving. Genii together may find themselves languishing in periods of inertia. Two Genii will, however, share a romantic attitude to life, although Genie men are sometimes too possessive for Genie women.

The Dragon: Genii and Dragons often clash. The overactive Dragon is just too disquieting for the Genie's peace of mind.

The Huntress: Huntresses tend to fall for Genii, although Genii may find the Huntress' way of living somewhat insecure for their liking.

Other Signs

Cascaya: Genii are romantics and the Cascayan loves anything adventurous. Many Genii make an eager audience for the charm and wit of the Cascayan.

Assari: In many ways the Genie shares a romantic and imaginative disposition with the Assari. The two signs may find that they clash if both trying to gain the attention of the same person or group. As partners, however, they often compliment one another, sharing many similar interests.

The Serpent: These two signs can share close friendships, although romantic attachments are less likely to succeed due to the Serpent's disconcerting inquisitiveness.

The Sphinx: The Genie loves a mystery and the Sphinx's life is often enigmatic. The Genie, however, likes to be treated as an equal and the Sphinx has an arrogant streak which many Genii dislike.

The Swallow: The Genie and Swallow share much in common and can enjoy each other's company. Close friendships and relationships may be problematic due to the Swallow's need for a more assertive partner.

Famous Genii

Tom Hanks. Born: 9 July 1956.

Tom Hanks has the typical charm of the Genie man. Like most Genii, he loves a challenge, often taking on the most difficult roles. Always eager for adventure, the Genie's life is full of surprises. With each new role, Tom Hanks brings something new and entertaining to the screen. Genii seldom grow bored, and Tom Hanks seems to genuinely enjoy every moment of his career. The Genie is an unyielding sign. Tom always makes certain that each role is his very own. The Genie is also a sign of compassion. Many of Tom's performances evidence a sympathetic insight into the life of the characters he plays.

Bill Cosby. Born: 12 July 1937.

As one of the best loved comedians, Bill Cosby has all the typical characteristics of the Genie man. Most Genii are popular and fun-loving, but behind it all there is a pure determination to succeed in whatever venture they decide to undertake. Consequently, Bill Cosby has not only earned himself international fame and recognition for his comedy, but he has also built up a one-man business empire.

Ginger Rogers. Born: 16 July 1911.

Many of the most successful dancers are born in the sign of the Genie. The darling of the silver screen, Ginger Rogers used her Genie imaginative and emotional performance skills in the most compelling way. Starring alongside Gene Kelly, Fred Astaire and other Hollywood greats, she dazzled audiences throughout the world with her natural Genie charm. Although at home in the limelight, her personal life was very much her own; privacy is much cherished by any Genie.

Fate and Fortune

Over the course of the year Genii can expect the following influences to affect their lives during the separate lunar cycles:

Cascaya: During the month of Cascaya Genii may need to spend time alone and reflect upon the circumstances surrounding them. Any new decisions taken at this time may need considerable thought.

The Phoenix: As the Phoenix month of renewal follows a month for the Genie to make plans, any new enterprise undertaken at this time is likely to reap rewards.

The Hero: The Hero and the Genie are signs that work well together. However, Genii may find that their imagination is not being allowed its full reign. Surprise offers of assistance can bring positive results.

Assari: Assari is a month of romance for the Genie. Many Genii find that during this cycle favourable relationships are formed. New opportunities arise in many areas of life, particularly concerning work or business matters. A month of good luck regarding anything concerning chance.

The Genie: Genii do not function at their best during their own month. They may find that they are unable to resolve difficulties or find ready solutions to problems. This may be a good time of the year for the Genie to take a vacation. Even a weekend away will probably do them the world of good.

The Griffin: For any Genie involved in business affairs, the Griffin month is favourable for sound financial decisions. Indeed, anything connected with monetary matters is favourably placed during this cycle. This is also a positive time for love and romance. Any Genie hoping for a new partnership may be pleasantly surprised during this cycle.

The Oryx: The swift Oryx brings news for the Genie. Old acquaintances may be renewed, although the Genie should be careful about new projects at this time.

Genii may find themselves taking too much at face value.

Etana: The Genie does not recover from disappointment as easily as some signs. If a Genie has suffered a setback they should deliberately try to involve themselves in something new. If matters are going the way the Genie hoped, they should be careful about making hasty or risky decisions.

The Serpent: The wise and learned Serpent brings much insight to the Genie during this month. Decisions concerning practical or domestic matters are likely to be well-founded. The Genie's insight into the motives and intentions of others is particularly astute during the Serpent month. Love, romance and affairs of the heart fare especially well for the Genie during this cycle.

The Dragon: Travel or change of home or work is favoured during the month of the flying Dragon. If the Genie intends to move house this can be a particularly advantageous time to start looking around. Similarly, if they have been thinking of changing their job then they could find this an especially advantageous month. If they are content to stay put, however, it is a good time for seeking promotion or expansion.

The Sphinx: This is a month of romance and adventure for the Genie. In most matters this is a favourable time, especially in love and leisure. A partner may also surprise the Genie. Generally, this is a month of the unexpected.

The Swallow: The Swallow can be the most adventurous month for the Genie. It may be a little *too* adventurous, however, as Genii may find themselves having far too much to handle. This is a particularly favourable month for forming new and lasting relationships or friendships. Important domestic or business decisions should be left until Genii have a little bit more time on their hands.

The Huntress During the Huntress month the Genie will find that their fortunes depend more on others than themselves. If the Genie is seeking relaxation then this is the ideal time for leisure pursuits. Any Genie whose life involves sport or physical recreation may find this a time of great success.

THE GRIFFIN

Approximate Calendar Month
AUGUST

Sign Chart Letter
F

THE GRIFFIN

THE Griffin was an ancient mythical beast with the head and wings of an eagle and the body of a lion. Like the Griffin, those born in this sign can be kings of the jungle and masters of the air. They can be creative and imaginative, yet retain a firm interest in practical affairs. They may be business people or artists, yet whichever profession they choose both these attributes are brought into play. Griffins are probably the most determined of all the signs, going through hell and high water to achieve their aims. Sometimes, however, they become headstrong and forge ahead like a rampaging lion.

Griffins are self-assured in most situations, and a natural capacity to take control affords them much respect. The Griffin has an air of authority, but unlike the Hero who needs to be seen to be in command, Griffins are quite prepared to work behind the scenes. To those born in this cycle it is the task that is important, not the person who carries it out.

For the Griffin, everything has its place. There is a time for work, a time for rest and a time for play. They commit themselves fully to each, but hate to mix the three. Griffins will devote themselves exclusively to whatever they are doing. They enjoy routine and keep regular habits. Meal times are observed with punctilious zeal, and sleep comes at the same hour every night. Griffins have a marvellous capacity to work hard all day, but once they have knocked-off for the evening their minds are tuned exclusively to relaxation. Without something specific to do, the Griffin is content to sit for hours, watching television, reading a book or listening to music. Like a gorged lion, Griffins enjoy their rest and do not take kindly to being disturbed.

Positive Characteristics

Griffins have a determined spirit with much capacity for creative thinking. They share a sympathetic and hospitable personality and spiritual aspirations are usually well-developed. Griffins have a generous nature and many exhibit an idealistic attitude to life. The common good is usually a high priority for the Griffin, who is prepared to make many a personal sacrifice to help those around them. Many Griffins have a philosophical attitude to life, and most have sublime faith that good will ultimately triumph.

Negative Characteristics

Relationships are sometimes made difficult by an obstinate spirit. There is a marked tendency to disregard the attitudes of others or to offend without intent. The Griffin will often consider every angle of a problem, which can lead to too much preparation and not enough action. Frequently, Griffins fail to seize opportunities offered them on a plate. Once they have found something to which they are committed, Griffin commitment is usually total. Consequently, although they are generally good with money, on personal ventures they may spend far more money than they can realistically afford.

Appearance

The Griffin's gaze is direct and benevolent. They have a habit of nodding knowingly when listening, and adopt an understanding smile – even when they are in complete disagreement. Griffins move with an air of confidence; they carry their heads high and walk with their backs straight. At rest, however, Griffins tend to sprawl. They seldom sit neatly in a chair, preferring to make the most of all available space and comfort. Few Griffins are quick or flighty, most being slow and deliberate movers.

Health

The Griffin ability to relax completely may result in weight problems. Few Griffins are worriers, and those born in this cycle are seldom concerned about their own well-being. Many are therefore inclined to ignore preventative medicine or disregard any tell-tale signs of illness. Repetitive strain injuries, or others such ailments which are best tackled early, may be left unattended by the Griffin. This can lead to complications which might easily have been avoided.

The Formula for Success

Griffins are unafraid of failure or recrimination. They are fully prepared to be disbelieved, even ridiculed, until their point is proven. Insults or sneers have little influence on Griffins, who have the confidence and self-assurance to believe they are right. Indeed, Griffins seldom commit themselves to any enterprise of which they are uncertain. Those born in this cycle are prepared to persevere long and hard to achieve results.

The good-natured and accommodating Griffin should not be mistaken as compliant. Those who consider the Griffin a pushover are in for a shock. Griffins usually know exactly what they want and how to get it. They may prefer to see others happy and contented, but should another's plan conflict with their own, Griffins will act forcibly and unyieldingly to prevail. Astuteness and strength of purpose work hand in hand to make the Griffin a formidable opponent.

Words of Advice

In legend the griffin was a guardian of hidden treasure. Like their mythical counterpart, those born in this sign are protective by nature. Once something is theirs they just hate to give it up. Griffins will adhere to a notion or continue with an enterprise even when it is outmoded or doomed to failure. They should take time to re-examine their circumstances and adjust their approach when necessary.

As the Griffin considers every factor before embarking on an enterprise, most endeavours are likely to succeed. However, if failure does result through unforeseen circumstances, the Griffin is usually ill-prepared. To avoid being left stranded, Griffins should remember to keep something in reserve. This advice is especially true in romance – love can be an all-or-nothing affair for the Griffin. If a relationship should fail the Griffin is taken completely off-guard. Although they may accept failure with dignity, it can strip them of the necessary determination to begin again. It will usually take someone or something else to spur them into action.

Suitable Occupations

Griffins flourish in many trades and professions. As keen planners and organizers they fare particularly well in commerce. An artistic Griffin has tremendous insight into what is popular; advertising and the world of fashion employs many a Griffin in important positions. Griffins are equally content to work behind the scenes. In the world of entertainment, for instance, as many Griffins are found off-stage as in the public eye. Those Griffins who do perform before an audience usually do so in a unique and unusual way.

Griffins in manual trades love to see an enterprise develop through every stage to completion. They have a desire to witness their direct contribution, so few Griffins are comfortable in a closed working environment.

The Griffin at Work

Griffins make considerate employers, exercising authority without becoming demonstrative or overbearing. They are always concerned for the well-being of their staff, and make certain that they are kept informed concerning all aspects of their work. Although Griffins make excellent bosses, they are not the best of entrepreneurs. In management, the Griffin lacks the ruthless streak sometimes necessary to make important financial decisions. Concern for their workforce is likely to preside over interests of sheer profit.

As employees Griffins make a positive contribution to the workforce. They are, however, inclined to side with those in difficulty, and the Griffin's willingness to defend an unpopular workmate can result in friction with other members of staff. Skivers and idlers may also feel uncomfortable in the Griffin's presence; it may seem that 'big brother' is always around. Those who are inclined to shirk their work-load may have reason to feel guilty, but no need to fear. The Griffin is a conscientious but loyal comrade, not the type to tell tales or go running to the boss.

The Griffin Woman

Griffins are sophisticated dressers, although they may be given to some rather unusual styles. Few women born in this cycle blindly follow fashion; they are usually trend-setters rather than followers. They are certainly not conservative in dress, although they may go for quality of clothing rather than variety, often preferring darker colours.

The Griffin woman is the most composed of any sign. She is assured, debonair, calm and collected, although not arrogant or aloof. Women born in some signs may deliberately desire to make their mark; to the Griffin, however, panache comes naturally. Although the Griffin woman is not flirtatious, she enjoys the attention of men. A certain intangible mystique turns many an eye in her direction.

Women born in this cycle are seldom loners, and most enjoy being part of a group. The Griffin woman likes to stand out in a crowd – not to stand alone. The one thing a Griffin woman cannot stand, however, is male chauvinism. She expects to be treated as an equal, and quickly finds an excuse to leave the company of the condescending male. Moreover, she hates seeing other women dominated by overbearing men. The Griffin woman is the first to offer support to a friend who finds herself the victim of male aggression.

As a career-woman the Griffin can be the most successful of signs. However, the Griffin woman likes to devote herself exclusively to whatever she is doing. Few born in this cycle have the desire to continue working once they have started a family.

The Griffin Man

The mythical Griffin was a guardian, and men born in this cycle have strong family ties. They are proud of their homes and of their family's achievements. They are the perfect providers but like their partners to concentrate on domestic affairs. The Griffin man may treat women well, but expects his partner's place to be in the home.

Once settled, Griffin men like to keep their home environment apart from the rest of their lives. At work the Griffin is a working man, at home he is a family man. He dedicates himself to each with equal commitment but hates to mix the two.

The Griffin man is a hoarder and, like the griffin of legend which jealously guarded its treasure, he is a collector of mementoes and memorabilia. In particular, he loves to keep a record of his life, and is often a keen photographer or home-video enthusiast. He is also a hobbyist, and most Griffins have some pet interest to occupy their spare time. They work, rest and play – but all have a set place and time. Sunday afternoon, for example, may be set aside for the gardening, a trip in the country or some other specific commitment. Beware of arriving at the Griffin's house unannounced – he will be most put out if his routine is disturbed. Make sure the Griffin has adequate warning of anything that may disrupt his life or necessitate a change of plan.

The Griffin Parent

The Griffin parent, although caring, is inclined to treat his or her family almost as a business venture. Griffin fathers have a tendency to act like firm but fair employers, while Griffin mothers are particularly concerned about their children's appearance. Both will ensure that their offspring are well looked after, but each has a tendency to concentrate too much on their children's physical well-being. To them, health, appearance, good manners and practical achievements are sometimes regarded to the exclusion of a child's emotional needs. The Griffin, however, is a benevolent and affectionate sign – they merely want the very best for their young.

The Griffin Child

Most Griffin children are relaxed in adult company, which some grown-ups may find disconcerting. They mature early, and seldom act the fool. From a very early age Griffins show a responsible and conscientious attitude to life. Griffin children work well in class but hate doing homework. Like their adult counterparts, they feel that once the working day is ended it is time to relax. Revising does not come easily, so examinations may suffer. If they enter higher education, however, their regulated life-style can prove extremely useful. Unlike some students who may skip lectures, Griffins will study long and hard from nine to five, as if they were already employed and paid to do a job.

The Griffin Friend

Loyalty is a Griffin virtue which stands undaunted in the face of crisis. Griffins will be especially staunch on a friend's behalf. They are idealists, always ready to come to the aid of others. Griffins handle criticism well and seldom take offence. Accordingly, they make easy-going friends, especially for those who are outspoken or temperamental. Excitability, erratic behaviour or changes of mood are taken in the Griffin's stride. All the Griffin asks of their friends is fairness and honesty. Griffins seldom hold a grudge and are quick to forgive – like the eagle, they soar high above the mundane.

Griffins do not show particularly sound judgement regarding those around them, however. They live as if in an ideal world and believe that others will act as considerately as they. Sadly, the world is not a perfect place and many Griffins suffer disappointments in business and personal relationships.

A prime Griffin fault is devotion to schedule. If the Griffin's time-table life is disturbed they are completely thrown. You will not always know when the obliging Griffin is upset. They may agree with your plans to disrupt their routine, only to spend the rest of the day repeatedly looking at their watch.

The Griffin Partner

The Griffin is affectionate and protective, although not romantic by nature. They look for home comforts in a relationship rather than matrimonial bliss. Both Griffin men and women seek partners who are homely and consistent. Griffin men seek devoted, domesticated wives, and Griffin women seek steady, reliable husbands.

Griffins throw themselves completely into a relationship, and naturally expect their partners to do the same. This, of course, will not always be so, particularly in the early days of dating. Such premature Griffin expectations are sometimes disturbing to other signs, who may need longer periods of acquaintance before making firm commitments. If Griffins did not seem so enthusiastic to marry and settle down, many a failed relationship may have developed quite differently. Griffins should always remember that partners often need more time.

Affinity Signs

The Oryx: The Griffin works particularly well with the Oryx. Oryx imagination can develop the Griffin's more practical ideas and both have considerable creativity. The two signs also compliment each other in business matters.

The Genie: Although Genii are romantic and fun-loving, they desperately need the kind of security the Griffin can offer. Griffins are not averse to romanticism, they simply need inspiration from signs like the Genie. These two signs compliment one another nicely.

Assari: The Griffin and the Assari are particularly compatible signs, especially concerning romantic affiliations. Both share common interests, whilst their personalities are sufficiently different not to clash.

The Swallow: The Griffin's strong family ties and protective instincts can make them ideal partners for Swallows. Swallows often look at life from a very different perspective to the Griffin, and their romantic imagination usually aids the Griffin's creativity.

Cascaya: Griffins are prepared to give others their own space – something the Cascayan desperately needs. Unlike some signs, the Griffin is usually an open book, having no problem with Cascayan inquisitiveness.

Problem Signs
The Griffin: Griffins often get on well with Griffins of their own sex. Romantic relationships may suffer, however. Griffin women find Griffin men far too chauvinistic regarding their ideas of marriage.

The Dragon: Dragons and Griffins share a similar creativity. However, the headstrong Griffin can often clash with the fiery temperament of the Dragon. Neither is prepared to give way to the other.

The Sphinx: In legend both the Griffin and the Sphinx

were treasure guardians. Those born in these signs often experience a clash of interests or personality. Sometimes they may even distrust one another.

Other Signs

The Phoenix: Phoenixes find Griffins too pragmatic. Although on a superficial level these two signs may tolerate one another, they seldom mix well as close companions.

The Hero: Griffins and Heroes mix well socially as both are polite and confident signs. When working together, however, there can be clashes of interest. In marriage there may be problems as both signs are exceptionally stubborn.

Etana: The Griffin and the Etana have few problems socially, although the Etana is seldom prepared to make the sort of long-term commitments the Griffin expects.

The Serpent: Griffins like to know precisely where they stand, and most find the Serpent difficult to fathom.

The Huntress: The Huntress can unnerve the Griffin. Few Griffins like ideas as unconventional as those many Huntresses appear to share.

Famous Griffins

Arnold Schwarzenegger. Born: 30 July 1947.

Those born in the sign of the Griffin are endowed with a number of varying attributes or abilities, often brought together in a chosen career. Arnold Schwarzenegger is a typical Griffin in this respect. He was a leading influence in the world of body-building long before he was ever a Hollywood superstar. Initially, acting did not come easily to Arnold but, like many born in this sign, he refused to quit. Griffins are probably the most determined of all the signs, going through hell and high water to achieve their aims.

Robin Williams. Born: 21 July 1952.

Like most Griffins, Robin Williams is creative and imaginative, yet retains a firm interest in material affairs. His zany sense of humour does not distract him from the practical considerations of what makes for popular entertainment. His talents as an actor and his multifarious character roles are typical of the Griffin's composite personality. Griffins may follow practical or artistic professions, yet whichever profession they choose all their various attributes are utilized. The Griffin's innovative abilities are well displayed in the inventive vigour which Robin brings to the characters he plays.

Madonna. Born: 16 August 1958.

The Griffin woman is by nature a trend-setter rather than a follower, and Madonna has been a leading setter of trends. Indeed, she has been a major influence in fashion. Her hairstyles, clothes, even her mannerisms have been copied by women throughout the world. As a performer, she has created a new genre that others have tried to emulate. Half measures are not to the Griffin's liking, and where possible those born in this sign make as big an impact as possible. It is hardly surprising, therefore, that Madonna has become not just another star but the queen of modern rock.

Fate and Fortune

Over the course of the year Griffins can expect the following influences to affect their lives during the separate lunar cycles:

Cascaya: Griffins are often frustrated by acquaintances who are not as far-sighted as they. During the elusive Cascaya month this can be particularly true. Griffins may find it especially hard to convince others of their ideas or point of view.

The Phoenix: The influence of the fiery Phoenix may result in headstrong reactions in Griffins. They should take care about saying more than they ought, lest they offend without intent.

The Hero: The Hero and the Griffin are both signs favourable for business and enterprise. In financial matters Griffins are often at their best during a Hero month. It is a time when hard work and dedication may finally pay off.

Assari: Together, the flying Griffin and the flying Assari bring much success in romantic pursuits and affairs of the heart. New friendships or relationships are possible and old acquaintances may be renewed. Few Griffins have problems during an Assari month. Even if difficulties should arise, Griffins are well placed to handle problems that befall them.

The Genie: The Griffin is both a practical and imaginative sign. The attributes of the adventurous Genie, when coupled with these natural Griffin traits, brings much success, particularly in matters concerning the arts. Social circumstances are also favoured during this month, as are sports, games and leisure activities.

The Griffin: Griffins work well during their own month, although friendships and relationships may suffer. Griffins could find themselves having to work so hard that they exclude their loved ones from their busy schedule.

The Oryx: For any Griffin in need of a vacation, now is the ideal time to get away.

Etana: In the cycle of Etana Griffins may profit by ignoring their usual reticence concerning risk ventures. It is a month of luck in matters of chance.

The Serpent: The Serpent is a sign of sudden or unexpected news for the Griffin. During this month the Griffin may be taken completely by surprise. For any Griffin seeking new friendships or partnerships this can be an especially favourable time.

The Dragon: For the Griffin, the fire-breathing Dragon brings imaginative insight. Griffins are likely to be inspired by new and fruitful ideas. This is a positive time for any change of job or location.

The Sphinx: This can be an emotional month for the Griffin. It is not the best time for important practical decisions, although it may be beneficial for love and romance.

The Swallow: The Swallow month is often the most uneventful in the Griffin's year. The delicate high-flying

Swallow is normally way out of reach for the Griffin – so also are progress and opportunity.

The Huntress: **Many Griffins find that the Huntress month brings luck and welcome news. It is a time of good fortune for most Griffins.**

THE ORYX

Approximate Calendar Month
SEPTEMBER

Sign Chart Letter
G

THE ORYX

ALTHOUGH a creature of the earth, the Oryx is a magical beast. Those born in this sign are both materialistic and imaginative, sharing much in common with the Assari, except that they keep their feet firmly on the ground. Whereas the Assari may be carried away with enthusiasm, the Oryx will continually review a situation. One of the chief characteristics of the Oryx is to constantly question the world about them. They are both analytical and self-critical, sometimes to the extent of impeding progress. However, the Oryx is the swiftest of creatures and once in the running they can achieve remarkable results in a very short time. Their charm, tact, and generosity, allied with a readiness to help others, play a large part in the Oryx's success.

Although possessing leadership qualities, Oryxes seldom make good leaders. Their interests can be so varied that they will change horses in mid-stream, and those who may have dropped everything to follow them can be left high and dry. This is not because Oryxes are insensitive; they naturally assume that others will be like themselves and update their interests if something more appropriate comes along.

Although Oryxes may express a keen interest in the arts, they rarely enjoy concerts or theatre, becoming restless when forced to remain seated for any length of time. Their own interests being original, Oryxes seldom join clubs or societies, preferring to create their own amusement.

Positive Characteristics

The Oryx has great versatility. Endowed with an alert mind and an excellent memory, the Oryx is capable of solving many problems that others find difficult. They are especially precise regarding minute detail; neat and methodical, they take pride in their work. In business, they work best alone, being capable of long periods of devoted activity. Philosophical interests are a marked feature, with considerable originality of ideas.

Negative Characteristics

If an enterprise fails, the Oryx may become oversensitive and quick to take offence. Pessimism is usual for Oryxes who have suffered a setback, and the response is generally to withdraw, accepting further problems as if they somehow deserve them. Although critical of themselves, they dislike being criticized by others and are usually the last people to take advice. Extravagance and impatience can lead to financial problems.

Appearance

Oryxes usually have an upright appearance, smooth complexion with warm, attractive eyes. Often large, the eyes are commonly the most striking feature of the Oryx. Oryxes tend to be slim with sharp or angular features. Like the Griffin, the Oryx retains a youthful appearance well into middle age. Even the worry lines that are likely to appear on their faces, make them look wiser rather than older.

Health

The parts of the body readily prone to infection are the stomach and abdomen; indigestion and intestinal difficulties are invariably complaints of this group. Nervous disorders may also be in evidence, and hypochondria is common. Leave them to browse through a medical dictionary and before long they think they're coming down with everything under the sun. Strangely enough, the Oryx is often the bravest sign when it comes to genuine illness. If they do fall sick or face injury, they cope well and may even continue with their normal routine against medical advice. However, the Oryx is a sign of good health and those born in this cycle are usually fit and trim.

The Formula for Success

In both social or business matters the Oryx's versatility can lead to much success, while their natural humour and acting skills help them fit into almost any situation. Moreover, they have the enviable talent of bringing out the best in others, making even the most mundane matters seem interesting. Exceptionally creative, the Oryx's ideas are often unconventional and original, attracting criticism from those who are less imaginative. The Oryx is one of the most analytical of signs, and many born in this cycle are capable of solving extremely difficult problems.

Words of Advice

As this is a sign of versatility, the Oryx should remain focused on one job at a time, rather than on numerous problems simultaneously. Their greatest drawback is that they have too many interests, ideas, and skills to devote themselves sufficiently to a single project. Their hypercritical side badly needs controlling, as does their touchiness about being criticized themselves. Extremely sensitive to criticism, the Oryx is often distracted or dissuaded by adverse opinion. They should concentrate more on what they are doing and worry less about what others may think. They must also learn to control their desire to overspend. Although their generosity is admirable, extravagance is always a risk. More than any other sign, money burns a hole in the Oryx's pocket.

Suitable Occupations

Writing professions, such as journalism, can be ideal for Oryxes as they have inquiring and critical minds. Other suitable professions entail abstract, statistical and inventive skills, such as computer-programming. Being natural entertainers, acting or performing of any kind can be a fitting career for the Oryx. They can also become accomplished musicians. Most of all, they make excellent lecturers, with inventive ways of making their subject-matter interesting. The Oryx works best in short, sharp bursts, however, and dislikes being tied down to rules and regulations.

The Oryx at Work

Oryxes are practical, industrious and conscientious about their work, being particularly methodical in the way they go about it. Walking encyclopaedias, the Oryx's hobbies are often related to their jobs. The Oryx's inability to relax means that, where possible, they take their work home with them. They have no intention of knocking-off the moment the working day ends. Unlike signs who find the thought of after-hours work disagreeable, the Oryx usually enjoys it.

The Oryx Woman

You will not catch an Oryx woman with her hair in curlers or slopping around the house in a dressing-gown. She always appears immaculate from the moment the day begins. Although she may spend less on her clothes than some other signs, she has good dress-sense, preferring classic styles. Her choice of colours are normally neutral – black, white, grey or brown.

Her home will be tastefully furnished and uncluttered, with a preference for light, open and airy rooms. The only cluttered place in her home, will be her medicine cupboard which is likely to be crammed with bottles of pills and a well-stocked first-aid kit. Like their male counterparts, Oryx women tend to be hypochondriacs.

The Oryx woman is not a collector of memorabilia, being the least nostalgic of any sign. Although not lacking a romantic streak, she nevertheless prefers to make the best of the here and now. What happens today is far more important than what happened yesterday. You rarely hear the Oryx saying 'I remember when . . .'.

Oryx women are practical and realistic regarding relationships. They never expect too much and are prepared to work towards a long and happy marriage. If a relationship fails, however, they are well-prepared to move on, providing they know that the situation is really hopeless. Seldom holding grudges, the Oryx woman does not infer rejection from the break-up of a relationship and copes well with matrimonial problems.

The Oryx Man

Although somewhat fussy or faddy, the Oryx man is a good socializer. At ease in the company of both sexes, he has an entertaining sense of humour and a versatile character, making him the soul of any party. However, the Oryx often gives the impression that he is not quite sharing the spirit of the occasion. Not that he appears rude or uninterested; rather, he is usually thinking of more than one thing at once.

The Oryx's intense dislike of aggression means that he will not allow himself to become involved in violence of any kind. If a social situation becomes unruly, men of this sign usually take their leave.

In domestic life the Oryx man is neat and tidy, unable to concentrate if he is surrounded by muddle. He makes a good husband for the woman who wants her partner to do his fair share of the housework. Taking great care to get to know his prospective partner well before plunging into marriage, the Oryx is usually faithful in a relationship, making certain that one has ended before another begins. He will not shirk his obligations to an ex-partner, neither will he knowingly be responsible for breaking up someone else's marriage.

The Oryx Parent

Oryxes make good parents and take a keen interest in their child's education. They bring up their children with concern and kindness, are seldom strict and refrain from any form of punishment unless absolutely necessary. The Oryx treats the child as they would treat an adult, always prepared to explain why something should be done in a particular way. Indeed, Oryxes set their children a good example with their tidy habits and considerate manners.

The Oryx Child

Oryxes can be difficult children. Although they seldom find themselves in serious trouble, and don't have a negative attitude to life, the Oryx child is hyperactive.

They rarely sit still and are always inquisitive. They are forever inventing new games to play and sometimes they will even break a toy, trying to modify it for some other purpose. Their creative imagination earns them many friends but often leads to quarrels with parents or elders. In short, the Oryx child can be extremely tiring.

Oryx children are hardly ever rude and are perhaps the most polite young people of any sign. Unfortunately, their sense of humour can get them into trouble, even though their pranks are not destructive, cruel or malicious. Paradoxically, the same good-humoured jesting by the Oryx adult often results in considerable popularity.

At school, the Oryx child may have the ability to be top of the class, but they are often distracted by their restless nature. 'Has the ability to do much better' or 'fools around in class' are often the words on their school reports. However, although they may not do so well during term-time, when it comes to examinations the Oryx invariably makes up for it, being capable of intensive revising.

Oryxes are good with pets and look after them well. Do not be surprised if they show a particular fondness for cats, for the cat and the Oryx have a great affinity. It is strange how often a stray will appear on the doorstep of the home of a Oryx child.

If a change of home or school should occur, the Oryx child is usually the last to worry. They are quick to make new friends and take care of themselves in most situations. The Oryx child is rarely aggressive, and in turn they are seldom bullied or badgered by other children. They hold their own by popularity and can live by their wits. Furthermore, Oryx versatility appears in childhood; the Oryx can be just as happy playing alone as with friends.

There is little danger that the Oryx teenager will experiment with sex at an early age, as they tend to be late developers in that respect. Conversely, Oryx children are seldom clingy and rarely experience difficulty leaving home when the time comes.

The Oryx Friend

Oryxes are generous and entertaining friends. Never short of new ideas, they are fun to be with; perhaps the best people with whom to share a night out. They are also a mine of information, having so many varied interests and experiences that they can keep you engrossed for hours. They are well-mannered and never cause embarrassment in mixed company.

Sometimes, however, Oryxes can be a trial. You may be feeling tired, or in need of peace and quiet, and along comes the Oryx with another great idea. Oryxes just can't relax: they have to keep busy, and see to it that you too are kept on the go. Although they have the best of intentions, there are times when the Oryx will be critical of their friends, expecting too much of others, even though they do offer constructive advice. Nevertheless, it must be acknowledged that Oryxes are hairsplitters, and quibble over minor matters of no real consequence.

Loyal though they are to their nearest and dearest, they are clear-sighted about the shortcomings of relatives, partners and close friends – and quick to remind them.

The Oryx Partner

One of the strangest Oryx traits is their failure to realize when they are attractive to a member of the opposite sex. It usually comes as a complete shock when they discover that someone is interested in them. This is often taken to be a lack of interest on the Oryx's part – a common and sometimes sad mistake. The Oryx man is particularly shy when it comes to starting a relationship, which is due to their own self-criticism rather than a lack of confidence. Although they worry too much and sometimes fail to act, Oryx men and women are generally caring and emotionally uninhibited once they have found the right partner.

Whether attractive or plain, both male and female Oryxes have an entertaining personality that often appeals to the opposite sex. However, Oryxes are usually bound up with their careers and are in no hurry to marry.

Affinity Signs

The Genie and Assari: The Oryx particularly enjoys the company of the Genie and Assari. The Genie's romanticism makes for an eager audience for the imaginative ideas of the Oryx. The Assari is also imaginative and together they inspire one another.

The Phoenix: The Phoenix ability to ignore the Oryx's mood swings or changes of direction makes long relationships possible.

The Griffin and The Oryx: The Oryx generally works best with Griffins and other Oryxes. The Griffin's creativity can develop the Oryx's ideas, while two Oryxes complement each other in business matters.

Problem Signs

The Hero and the Serpent: The Serpent and the Hero are generally signs where the Oryx finds greatest difficulty. Both leadership signs, they enjoy taking charge too much for Oryx's liking. The Hero is often too bossy, while the Serpent – in the Oryx's opinion – is an inquisitive busybody.

Cascaya: The Oryx likes privacy too much to be constantly around the inquisitive Cascaya. The Cascaya often finds fault with the Oryx's changeability. Cascayans themselves are changeable, but in activities and not, as Oryxes can be, in temperament.

The Sphinx: The Sphinx is the sign that the Oryx finds hardest to fathom. Their ability to make something out of nothing, and their keen financial sense, are mysteries to the Oryx.

Other Signs

Etana: Etanas can make good acquaintances, being inspired by the Oryx, yet they do not necessarily make ideal partners. The Oryx lacks the romantic affection that the Etana needs.

The Dragon: The Dragon's optimism and will to succeed is admired by the Oryx, although they may become frustrated by the Dragon's failure to see the obvious.

The Swallow: The Oryx is often attracted to the openness of the Swallow, although the Oryx can mentally exhaust the Swallow who prefers a more serene lifestyle.

The Huntress: Although the Huntress and the Oryx mix well socially, relationships or business partnerships can suffer. When together, they tend to behave irresponsibly.

Famous Oryxes

David Copperfield. Born: 16 September 1956.

Who better to typify the magical Oryx than world-famous magician David Copperfield. As an illusionist, David employs both the practical and imaginative Oryx traits. The conjuror needs to utilize all the creative talents of the stage performer, but at the same time retain an expertise in the down-to-earth mechanics of his art. Most born in the cycle of the Oryx are analytical in their professional lives. David is the perfect example of an Oryx using all his critical faculties to create a spellbinding performance. Like all successful magicians, David needs to continually re-examine his ever-changing show in order to thrill his audience. Above all the conjuror needs to be original, and originality is a prime Oryx trait.

Richard Gere. Born: 31 August 1949.

Oryx longevity of youth is particularly apparent in the face of actor Richard Gere. He has the typical smooth appearance of this sign, and his warm Oryx eyes are one of his most striking features. Oryxes retain a youthful appearance well into middle age and, like many men of this sign, Richard's grey hair has simply added to his distinguished image. Like most Oryxes, Richard has a sophisticated and popular manner. Many Oryxes who can afford it lead an extravagant and glamorous life-style, and Richard is no exception.

Britt Ekland. Born: 6 October 1942.

Another who shares the ageless magic of the Oryx is actress Britt Ekland. She has reached her fifties with the brightness and sparkle of a woman two decades younger. Like most Oryx women, Britt always appears immaculate, preferring classic styles of dress, usually of a neutral colour. It is not only her looks and enviable figure that has made Britt so famous. With natural charm and charisma, she has become one of the most popular guests on television chat shows. Like many born in this sign, her good humour and vitality are contagious. Oryxes love adventure and excitement. Indeed, Britt has become one of the world's most notorious jet-setters. Typical of the Oryx, her flamboyant personality does not detract from the sophistication of this sign.

Fate and Fortune

Over the course of the year Oryxes can expect the following influences to affect their lives during the separate lunar cycles:

Cascaya: Strangely, the month of Cascaya is often a time when the Oryx bumps into people they prefer not to meet. It can also be a time of unwelcome news and upset plans. Many Oryxes will not be unhappy when the cycle of Cascaya is complete.

The Phoenix: During the month of the Phoenix many Oryxes will be ready for something different in their lives. New opportunities, particularly in social circumstances, are likely. It is also a favourable time for romance.

The Hero: During the month of the Hero the Oryx is particularly astute in their approach to most endeavours. It is a time of sound judgement, and many Oryxes will benefit from important decisions made during this cycle. This is their luckiest month for anything involving chance.

Assari: Assari is a sign of reluctance or hesitation concerning fresh endeavours. The Oryx, being a particularly analytical and self-critical sign, may be too cautious in this month. Oryxes are likely to change their minds repeatedly during this cycle. It is probably the best time of year to take a vacation.

The Genie: For the Oryx the Genie is the message-bearer and good news is likely. If the Oryx is considering a change of home or occupation now may be a favourable time to start looking.

The Griffin: It is often during the month of the Griffin that the Oryx is at their best regarding monetary or business matters. Oryxes are not materialistic by nature, but the Griffin tends to focus their attention on the practical details of life. This is also a good month for sport and leisure activities.

The Oryx: During their own sign the Oryxes are at their most self-critical. They may be inclined to concede defeat rather too readily. Relationships and friendships may suffer due to Oryx self-recrimination.

Etana: The month of Etana, more than any other sign, is a time of new opportunities in romantic or adventurous affairs for the Oryx. It is often their most successful month in any endeavour and new opportunities are likely. Oryxes are frequently inspired and quick to seize the initiative at this time of year.

The Serpent: The Serpent can open many unexpected

doors in the Oryx's life. Even if problems do occur the Oryx is well-placed to divert them to their advantage.

The Dragon: The month of the Dragon is a cycle of high activity for the Oryx. They should be careful not to overwork themselves. Oryxes can become touchy or oversensitive to the opinions of others. The Oryx may need to spend time alone during the Dragon month.

The Sphinx: Oryxes are generally extravagant by nature. During the month of the Sphinx they tend to spend more than they should. It is also a time during which the Oryx throws caution to the wind. The Oryx loves a mystery, and the riddle of the Sphinx may prove disastrous if attempted but unsolved. An accepted challenge may well backfire at this time of the year. Caution is certainly the better part of valour for the Oryx during the month of the Sphinx.

The Swallow: In Babylonian mythology the Swallow was an omen of good fortune. This is particularly true for the magical Oryx. During this month most Oryxes find that something long awaited will finally materialize. Any Oryx seeking new romantic attachments may find this month particularly eventful.

The Huntress: The Huntress is specifically a sign of love and romance as far as the Oryx is concerned. Successful Oryx relationships are very often formed during the month of the Huntress.

ETANA

Approximate Calendar Month
OCTOBER

Sign Chart Letter
H

ETANA

IN Babylonian legend Etana was a quest hero who chose to embark upon the greatest adventure of all – a journey to the gods themselves. To reach their realm, Etana flew high on the back of a giant eagle and he is often represented by an eagle. Like their mythical counterpart, Etanas often take risks or embark upon an enterprise without fear. When their risks pay off, however, great success is possible. Ignoring the sneers of others, their reward is often 'I told you so'. Those born in the sign of Etana are stubborn in their convictions, although they make loyal and trustworthy friends. Being so inventive, those born in this sign tend to be absent-minded and are forever losing their personal possessions or mislaying important items.

Etanas are always prepared for a new challenge; they love variety, and nothing unusual or unexpected catches the Etana off guard. Etanas have extreme confidence in their endeavours, and so disasters are seldom anticipated. Although at their best during a difficult, up-hill struggle, Etanas find it hard to pick themselves up and start again if disaster should strike.

Etanas are essentially good-natured and considerate, although of a highly-charged disposition. They are motivated by the urge to extract the best from life, as much by adapting themselves to existing conditions as by creating new possibilities. Unlike the Griffin, another determined sign, Etanas do not attempt to bull-doze their way through obstacles, but skilfully navigate their way around them.

Positive Characteristics

The Etana is the most expressive of signs. They are inventive and creative, having equal artistic and technical flair. The Etana is forever formulating fresh ideas. Always on the look out for something new, they are prepared to take risks courageously. Not easily distracted, those born in the Etana sign have an optimistic attitude towards most endeavours. They share an emotional and romantic temperament, coupled with a keen interest in the well-being of others. Many are considerate and trustworthy, with a strong sense of loyalty toward those they love. Etanas are blessed with an abundance of originality and permit little to stand in the way of a fruitful and interesting life-style.

Negative Characteristics

An unrealistic attitude to life can make it difficult for Etanas to realize ambitions. Complications can arise through failure to accept problems or avoid danger. Many Etanas have a stubborn attitude, sometimes amounting to pig-headedness. Conflict with those in authority or incompatibility in family life is often a problem for Etanas. They tend to be extravagant with money and in business matters mistakes are likely to be made with investments. Although the Etana takes courageous risks, they do not recover easily from failure. Most endeavours are all or nothing for the Etana, and few born in this cycle leave anything in reserve.

Appearance

The arms are one of the most notable features of the Etana. They are long and graceful, and Etanas tend to use them expressively in conversation, making wide and exaggerated gesticulations. Etana is not the neatest of signs. Unless it is essential to dress up for an occasion, most born in this cycle are content to wear whatever is at hand.

Health

One problem that many Etanas share is insomnia. Few Etanas sleep deeply or for long, and restless nights are common for this sign. This is especially true if the Etana is engaged in a particularly absorbing enterprise. Sometimes stress and long periods of devoted activity can lead to headaches or migraines. For the Etana who has suffered a setback, there is a marked tendency toward melancholia or even depression.

The Formula for Success

Flying on the back of a giant eagle, the legendary Etana had a panoramic view of the world. Similarly, those born in this sign share an overall appreciation of an endeavour in which they are engaged. Few are specialists by nature, preferring instead to involve themselves in most aspects of an enterprise. Although they may be 'Jacks of all trades', Etanas always ensure that they master the most important aspect of their work to the full. The typical Etana is always prepared to take risks to ensure success. Many Etanas are the first to break new ground, and two prime Etana traits are dedication to work and adaptability to fresh ideas.

Words of Advice

Exceptionally creative, the Etana's ideas are often unconventional and original, attracting adverse criticism from those who are less imaginative. Few Etanas, however, will accept censure without a fight. Although others may hold unconventional views in private, most Etanas say what they feel and express what they believe. This may lead to conflicts which could otherwise have been avoided. Etanas should learn to hold their tongues now and again, and try a little harder to impress or even flatter those whose help they need. For the Etana, what happens today is far more important than what happened yesterday; they desperately need change and variety. This may result in an avoidance of responsibility, and severing of ties that may later be needed. Etanas should avoid burning the bridges they have crossed.

Suitable Occupations

Many athletes, needing repeatedly to break the pain barrier or to push themselves beyond endurance, are born in this sign. Etanas are often ground-breakers, such as astronauts, test pilots and those in the field of dangerous pioneering work. Where there is hazard you will find the Etana. Fire-fighters, police, aid-workers and coastguards: so often, it is those born in this sign who are prepared to put their lives on the line to help others in danger.

Etanas can make extremely successful politicians, easily handling the multifarious skills necessary for the role. They have excellent communicative abilities, and an attention-grabbing and persuasive form of expression. Few Etanas fail to argue their point.

As artists or musicians Etanas are particularly creative, although there is a marked tendency to use their creative talents for disseminating a message rather than employing art for its own sake. As managers or employers Etanas may not always be the best of signs. They may lead far too readily from the front and fail to offer the support and encouragement that others may need.

The Etana at Work

As a negotiator, the persistent Etana excels. Bargaining can be a long and arduous affair and the Etana is an able player at the waiting game. Those who believe that they are getting the better of any deal with Etanas are deluding themselves. Etanas go through hell and high water to achieve their aims. Many Etanas are self-made people, having a highly personal style. However, headstrong emotions can send them forging ahead and others may find it difficult to keep pace. Many Etanas have an eccentric personality which workmates will either love or hate. There is seldom room for anything in between with the Etana. Etanas make good allies but bad opponents. Successful working relations very much depend upon being on the Etana's good side.

The Etana Woman

Fashion sense does not come naturally for many Etana women. To those born in this sign, what they are doing is far more important than how they look. The Etana woman is prepared to dress well to suit an occasion or to conform at work. However, she looks her best in casual attire. A clean but scruffy look can suit her down to the ground, giving her an aura of relaxed confidence. Few Etana women feel comfortable if dressed to the nines.

The Etana woman can be the toughest of any sign. It is not that she lacks femininity; so determined is she to make her mark in the world, that feminine poise is a low priority. She is a good socializer and is usually popular with other women – over whom she can exert much influence. Men may find her somewhat daunting, as she controls the men in her life with little difficulty. Few women born in this cycle would suit the domineering male. The Etana picks out the man she wants and pursues him with determination.

The Etana not only makes an excellent career woman but also a caring mother. With an abundance of mental energy, she can easily handle her working and family responsibilities together. She does not take eagerly to housework, however, and will expect her partner to do his fair share. Everything in her home may appear to be neat and tidy, but if you look carefully you'll discover her secret: children's toys kicked under the bed, dust brushed under the carpet and dirty laundry shoved in a cupboard.

The Etana can be a great asset to her partner's career. If she does not have one of her own, she is impelled to involve herself in his. She will be the perfect guest or hostess at business dinners, and will make certain to forge her own social connections which will benefit her partner's career.

The Etana Man

Like his female counterpart, the Etana male is imaginative, witty and erudite. However, he is not every girl's idea of the perfect date. He can be marvellous company, full of anecdotes, jokes and fun. However, he has an unusual, sometimes eccentric manner which can be a bit intimidating for some women. Moreover, he says exactly what he thinks, which may not always be what his partner wants to hear. Luckily, he prefers women with an unconventional attitude to life – few others can take the Etana man in their stride.

In legend Etana was a quest hero, similar to Gilgamesh, the champion of the Hero sign. The two signs accordingly share common traits. Both are adventurous, although the Hero is far more pragmatic. Both are leaders by nature, but whereas the Hero will ensure that his followers are ready and able, the Etana just expects them to follow. The Etana seems unaware that others may have difficulty keeping pace. In legend the hero Etana eventually decided to fly to heaven itself, and few beside those born in this sign are prepared to go where angels fear to tread.

The Etana man is more of a gambler than the woman of this sign. He cannot resist the temptation of trying to make money the easy way. Concerning financial matters in general, the male Etana lacks the thrift of the female. He is often late with his bills and all too willing to obtain credit that he cannot afford to repay. However, the Etana is luckier than many signs – his excesses sometimes pay off.

The Etana Parent

Etanas are affectionate though not possessive parents. Their children are encouraged to be self-reliant and to mix freely with others. They like to be considered as friends to their kids, and many children of Etanas enjoy their parent's company throughout much of their lives. Etana parents often look forward to school vacations; they can engage themselves in thinking of interesting and absorbing pastimes to enjoy with their children. Neither Etana mothers nor fathers suffer from the common problem of expecting too much of their young. They may have unrealistic ambitions for themselves, but these harsh expectations are seldom inflicted on their children.

The Etana Child

The Etana child is the most contrary of any sign. From an early age they are forever disagreeing with teachers or parents. It is no good merely telling an Etana child that something simply is; you will always be faced with an abrupt 'Why?'. Many Etana children are hyperactive which, coupled with their natural inquisitiveness, can make them something of a handful. The questioning Etana is quick to learn, however, and providing their curiosity is accommodated they can be as entertaining as their adult counterparts.

Many children are untidy but Etanas are especially so. On the positive side, they are generally concerned about the well-being of others, and few Etana children will be cruel or unkind. In fact they have a sympathetic attitude to others right from infancy, and are sometimes far too ready to offer assistance and help. When in trouble, children have a tendency to deny responsibility and accuse a friend or sibling. The Etana child, however, is usually willing to admit fault, and may even take the blame on behalf of friends.

The Etana Friend

Etanas are tremendous fun to have around. They share a marvellous, although unusual, sense of humour, live life to the full and can be the soul of any party. They have an abundance of energy, love being the centre of attention and have a great aptitude to think up novel and interesting schemes. However, the Etana can be somewhat draining – they never seem to stop. For some signs the Etana is best in small doses. Others who enjoy the unusual are often at their happiest in the company of the exciting Etana. But beware! The Etana also expects to share their problems. With most born in this sign, friendship is an all-or-nothing affair.

Etanas are quick to forgive and seldom hold a grudge – unless, that is, someone has deliberately done them harm. When Etanas have what they believe to be a justifiable grievance, they are expert at exacting revenge. They can stir up trouble for their enemies by skilfully setting others at their throats, while all the time remaining apparently blameless themselves.

Etanas often relocate frequently during the course of their life, few being content to remain in one place or situation for long. The Etana may have much to say but they hate reminiscing. Etanas live for today and tomorrow. The past is passed, and old times have little interest for most Etanas.

The Etana Partner

Etanas have no inclination to feign an interest in matters which fail to absorb them. If they are bored they will say so. This can sometimes lead to conflicting behaviour in the caring Etana. If impelled by circumstances to be involved in something in which they have no real interest, they consider it a tiresome, duty-bound responsibility. Consequently, they will carry out what is expected of them, but make certain that everyone knows exactly how they feel. It is often advisable for a partner to exclude an Etana from anything in which they have no enthusiasm. Unlike some signs who may hate feeling left out of anything, the Etana will quite happily apply themselves to something else.

The Etana is a complainer, especially about the service in hotels, restaurants or shops. Indeed, on occasions, especially during journeys and vacations, Etanas can be a right pain with their grouching and moaning. It is usually a good idea for an Etana's partner to handle receptionists, waiters and other serving staff – it will certainly make life easier for everyone concerned.

Etanas may not be the most romantic of partners for a date, but they desperately need love in their lives. They are a particularly caring sign, have a deeply sentimental streak, and need and offer true affection. They may say exactly what they feel, they may be inclined to moan, but Etanas fall madly in love and will make many a personal sacrifice to ensure their partner's happiness. Etanas may be individualists but they are certainly not loners.

Affinity Signs

Cascaya: Both signs are particularly tolerant of one another. The Etana's shortcomings are similar to the Cascayan's own, such as escaping wherever possible from tiresome responsibilities. Both hate to feel restricted. With so many interests, Etanas seldom find themselves in conflict with Cascayans.

The Genie: Etanas are often admired by the Genie for their originality and courageous attitude to life. Strong attachments are possible and relationships are usually successful. The Etana can bring many interesting opportunities into the Genie's life, whereas the Genie's down-to-earth approach, particularly to financial matters, protects the Etana from dangerous excess.

The Serpent: Although Serpents and Etanas are opposites in many respects, their traits and attributes are complimentary. The Serpent is patient and plans long and hard; the Etana is impetuous. The Serpent can restrain the Etana, while the Etana can bring more spontaneity to the Serpent's life.

The Sphinx: Etanas and Sphinxes often mix well. The Sphinx has many ideas which they lack the courage to try. The Etana is quite prepared to implement the Sphinx's schemes. These signs often make ideal partners in marriage.

Problem Signs

The Phoenix: Potentially the most problematic sign for the Etana is the Phoenix. The Phoenix can recover well from failures, but the Etana finds it hard. Both signs are adventurous, but when the Phoenix burned it rose again. The two signs get on great to begin with, but should problems occur the Phoenix cannot understand the Etana's inability to cope.

The Dragon: The energetic Dragon and the flighty Etana will often argue and bicker even when they see eye-to-eye.

The Swallow: The serenity of life-style the Swallow needs is unlikely to be found in close proximity to the Etana.

Other Signs

The Oryx: Although the Oryx can make a good acquaintance, they do not necessarily make ideal partners for the Etana. The Oryx lacks the romantic affection that the Etana needs.

The Hero: The Etana is a particularly affectionate sign, and the Hero tends to distrust open displays of affection. The Hero, however, can sometimes provide an emotional balance for the Etana.

Assari: Etanas and Assaris both allow their imaginations a free reign. Consequently, the two signs get on well but may behave irresponsibly when together.

The Griffin: The Griffin and the Etana have few problems on a social level, although the Etana is seldom prepared to make the sort of long-term commitments the Griffin may expect.

Etana: Two Etanas together usually behave in a completely impractical manner. Financial and other material considerations are usually ignored by wives and husbands alike if both are Etanas. In social circumstances, however, Etanas are usually fascinated by each other's attitude to life; they are ever ready to enjoy each other's company.

The Huntress: As both Etanas and Huntresses commit themselves so completely to a chosen pursuit, these two signs work well together if they share a similar heart-felt interest. If their interests lie in different directions, however, they are unlikely to have the time to spare for one another.

Famous Etanas
John Cleese. Born: 27 October 1939.

John Cleese is born into a sign of determination, having gone through hell and high water to achieve his aims. Many Etanas are self-made people, and John has made a unique place for himself in the world of comedy with an idiosyncratic style. However, his headstrong emotions can send him forging ahead of those around him, who may find it difficult to keep pace. The eccentricity of many Etanas is particularly evident. Yet although his sense of humour has made him one of the world's most popular comedians, he also shares the serious, principled side of the Etana; a combination of humour and intellect which often leads the Etana to achieve ground-breaking success. John has a determined spirit coupled with the usual Etana capacity for creative thinking.

Margaret Thatcher. Born 13 October 1925.

The typical Etana is always prepared to take risks to assure success. Politically courageous, Margaret Thatcher was one of the most prolific Prime Ministers in British history. Many Etanas are the first to break new ground, and Lady Thatcher was not only one of the first women to lead a major western democracy, but she became the leader of the most traditional of the British political parties. Two prime Etana traits are dedication to work and adaptability. As a politician Margaret Thatcher was exceptionally hard-working and soon adapted to her centre role on the world stage. Etanas make good friends, but bad enemies, and Lady Thatcher is either loved or hated. There is seldom room for anything in between with the Etana.

John Lennon. Born: 9 October 1940.

Remarkably creative, the Etana's ideas are often unconventional and original, attracting adverse criticism from those who are less imaginative. John Lennon was often the subject of media fault-finding and, typical of this sign, he would not accept censure without a fight. Although others may hold unconventional views in private, John, like most Etanas, said what he felt and expressed what he believed. Etanas are especially inventive, and John Lennon became an innovative cult-hero the world over. For the Etana, what happens today is far more important than what happened yesterday; they desperately need change and variety. John Lennon lived one of the most diverse lives of any star.

Fate and Fortune

Over the course of the year Etanas can expect the following influences to affect their lives during the separate lunar cycles:

Cascaya: During the month of the intangible Cascaya the Etana's plans may prove impractical. They may find themselves out of touch with everyday events, and relationships or social occasions may suffer from the Etana's unrealistic expectations.

The Phoenix: The resourceful Phoenix brings many new opportunities for the Etana. At no other time of the year is the Etana so ready to succeed, especially in commercial ventures.

The Hero: The practical Hero has a positive effect on Etanas and imaginative enterprises can come to fruition. New relationships or business links formed at this time may prove positive for the Etana. Love, romance and affairs of the heart are particularly well-favoured during this month.

Assari: During this month the Etana is often at their most adventurous. Their fun-loving disposition is best directed toward leisure activities, and many Etanas will find a vacation exhilarating. Any Etana on the lookout for new romantic attachments may be pleasantly surprised during this cycle.

The Genie: Domestic situations are well-placed during the month of the Genie. New opportunities for expansion or relocation may present themselves around the end of this cycle. It may also be a particularly advantageous time for the Etana considering a change of occupation.

The Griffin: The month of the Griffin is when the Etana is likely to make errors of judgement. The headstrong Griffin and Etana influences combined can result in a lack of tact or restraint by the Etana.

The Oryx: The Oryx is the message bearer for the Etana. During this month Etanas can expect favourable news.

Etana: During their own month Etanas are especially reckless. They should think long and hard about any change of direction they may be considering. If an enterprise is firmly established, however, a favourable turn of events is likely – provided that the Etana lets events be as they are.

The Serpent: The quick-fire Serpent brings the Etana a period of much success in social and leisure activities. Sporting events are particularly favoured at this time. Indeed, games of any kind can be enjoyed to the full, often with remarkable success. A lucky month for risk ventures.

The Dragon: Anything concerning group activities, either social or business in nature, is well-placed for the Etana. Etanas who take the initiative at this time of the year is likely to find themselves in a profitable position. This may be the most romantic month of the year for those born in the sign of Etana.

The Sphinx: It is the Sphinx's guardian role that engages for the Etana during this month. Nearly everything the Etana tries to accomplish seems to be prevented, and all the Etana hopes for seems to be delayed.

The Swallow: The month of the Swallow often brings a well-earned rest for the Etana. It is the time of year they can most easily relax. Etanas engaged in outdoor activities will find it a particularly fruitful time.

The Huntress: The Huntress is a sign of change for the Etana, particularly change of location. Some Etanas may be impelled to move during the month of the Huntress. Exciting and promising opportunities are also on the cards.

THE SERPENT

Approximate Calendar Month
NOVEMBER

Sign Chart Letter
I

THE SERPENT

THE Serpent has long been a symbol of knowledge, and those born in this sign often exude an aura of wisdom. They have logical and calculating minds, formulating plans and waiting patiently for the precise moment to act. Although they enjoy the virtue of patience, they live constantly in a state of readiness. Like the snake, they strike instantly when the time is right. Serpents are dedicated and conscientious workers. They are eager to learn and quick to find practical applications for their knowledge. Observant and with a keen eye for the minutest of details, the Serpent seldom misses a trick. Frequently it is the Serpent who is called upon to deal with the problems others have failed to solve. Serpents are avid readers, preferring factual rather than fictional works. The novels they do read tend to be more serious in content than those enjoyed by other signs.

Serpents are prepared to work long and hard to achieve their objectives. They are highly ambitious, seldom deterred by adversity and almost oblivious to hostile opinion. Although Serpents share a pragmatic and materialistic attitude to life, they approach nothing in a dull or tedious fashion. Indeed, most Serpents ooze enthusiasm for their chosen subjects. They may be given to high-spirited and frivolous behaviour in their spare time, but during working hours they are serious and determined. Serpents are realists, directing their energy toward their endeavours with logic and common sense, rather than – what they would consider – lofty intuition.

Positive Characteristics

Serpents have a serious outlook on life, coupled with a strong sense of responsibility. They are prepared to let their hair down and enjoy themselves, but only at the right time and when their working day has ended. Their ambition is supported by a shrewd intellect and the ability to devote themselves exclusively to an enterprise. Observant and inquisitive, the Serpent is quick to learn. They are especially loyal to their friends and take family values seriously. Mental energy is a marked feature of those born in this sign, together with a direct and decisive manner. Many Serpents show considerable initiative in the handling of financial affairs. They have swift analytical minds and are capable of solving complex problems. With strong will-power and great determination, the self-motivated Serpent is a force to be reckoned with.

Negative Characteristics

A cynical temperament may restrict social activities. Often too ready to disregard the opinions of their acquaintances, arrogance is sometimes a Serpent fault. Occasionally, Serpents share a less than sympathetic attitude to others. They seem to think that everyone can handle adversity as easily as themselves. Serpents also have a tendency to take themselves much too seriously at times, finding it hard to stand back and laugh at their mistakes. They are slow to forgive those who have offended them, and many Serpents are inclined to hold grudges for far too long. The Serpent is economically-minded and may be over-thrifty at times.

Appearance

Like the head of a swaying cobra, Serpents will use their hands as a prominent means of expression. If they disagree, they will slice their hands through the air as if to cut the conversation dead; in anger, they will stab an accusing finger in their opponent's direction; and when they have had enough, they will thrust out their palms to call for silence. There is also a serpentine quality to their behaviour. A snake will remained coiled and motionless for hours until their prey draws near – then they strike. At rest, those born in the Serpent sign will be calm and serene. When they spring into action, however, they are fast, efficient and effective. Some snakes are said to mesmerize their prey; many Serpents have melodic voices possessing an almost hypnotic quality.

Health

The Serpent is especially susceptible to coughs and colds. If a flu virus is going around the Serpent is sure to catch it. Cold, damp weather also plays havoc with those born in this sign. They thrive in the hottest of climates, whereas if it is chilly or wet the Serpent is likely to suffer. Rheumatism, arthritis and similar complaints may be a problem for Serpents, especially in later years.

The Formula for Success

The Serpent is one of the most objective of signs. Those born in this cycle refuse to judge a book by its cover. They seldom, if ever, jump to conclusions about anything. Even when dealing with someone they dislike, they will not allow prejudice to cloud their judgement. Able to ignore irrelevant faults, Serpents always respect and utilize the positive traits of allies and opponents alike. Few Serpents hold strong likes and dislikes. Their opinions are usually founded upon logic, not sentiment.

Serpents exercise enviable patience concerning most endeavours and accurately judge the correct moment to act. They also have the capacity to grasp the root of a problem, possessing shrewd insight into the real cause of difficulties they may face. In any enterprise the Serpent will weigh up its potential long and hard before making decisions. Serpents are forthright and astute, they have inquiring and probing minds and are remarkably self-disciplined.

Words of Advice

Serpents can be far too cynical at times, refusing to believe anything which has not been proved beyond reasonable doubt. They are unlikely to take anything on face value or on someone else's word. Serpents should try to have a little more faith in human nature. This may not be a perfect world, but others are generally more honest than the Serpent is prepared to give them credit.

Another Serpent trait is the need to know the detailed affairs of those around them. Sometimes Serpents are just too inquisitive for their own good. However, Serpents are themselves secretive. Few Serpents will reveal their own motivations, feelings and intentions. Serpents would make excellent poker players if they were inclined to gamble. To Serpents, however, anything based chiefly upon luck is strictly a mug's game. The Serpent should learn to take the occasional risk.

Suitable Occupations

Serpents make especially good entrepreneurs, managers or supervisors. They watch and listen carefully before arriving at conclusions, and only do so after every angle has been considered. Accordingly, they make solid judgements and usually take sound commercial decisions. Furthermore, they are quick to assert authority in a firm, decisive manner.

Occupations involving intricate, detailed or complex calculations are ideal for Serpents. They work well with figures and excel in financial careers. Architects, designers and engineers also include many successful Serpents amongst their ranks. Their keen eye for detail also suits the Serpent for work involving proofreading, editing or copywriting. Serpents are also found in academic and teaching occupations, and in anything involving investigation or research.

The Serpent at Work

Some signs may find it hard to apply themselves to difficult or arduous tasks. Serpents, however, apply themselves with remarkable dedication. They have the enviable ability to concentrate fully on whatever they are doing. Employers can always rely on the Serpent to do their job to the best of their ability. Snakes are solitary hunters, and the same goes for many born in the Serpent sign. They sometimes find it difficult to socialize with those with whom they work. Indeed, they may keep their working colleagues quite separate from their social lives.

The Serpent Woman

Whatever the Serpent woman puts her mind to she carries out in a responsible, determined and dedicated manner. She makes an ideal career woman, but will seldom return to work once she has started a family. The Serpent will devote herself exclusively to whatever she is doing. She can be an accomplished career woman and a devoted housewife but is unlikely to mix the two.

The Serpent is a creature of thrift and economy. This is particularly true of the Serpent woman. Whether or not she is a follower of fashion will depend very much on her chosen life-style. She is a smart dresser and takes pride in her appearance, but has no intention of laying out good money to buy trendy clothes for the sheer sake of it. If her work necessitates a fashionable image, however, she will go to considerable lengths to make certain she is second to none. The Serpent hostess, actress or model, for instance, will ensure she is wearing the very best and latest style. Indeed, Serpents make some of the most successful women whose working life is spent in the public eye or before the camera.

The Serpent Man

The Serpent is a sociable man but refuses to involve himself in irrelevant small-talk. He is sparing with his affections; others usually need to share his sentiments before he is prepared to commit himself to friendship. With his friends and loved ones the Serpent is a mine of fascinating information. Not only will he know his pet subject inside out, he will air his opinions in the most entertaining manner.

Like his female counterpart, the Serpent man is keen on physical fitness. He may be a regular visitor to the gym, swimming-pool or squash court, but he is unlikely to be an ardent supporter or spectator. The

Serpent man has little enthusiasm for sporting events in which he has no personal stake. Many Serpent men are more concerned with business affairs than leisure-time activities. Like the career woman of this sign, the Serpent man believes that business is business. He may even be ruthless in his commercial dealings. He expects his competitors and rivals to be as hardened as he. The Serpent man is a shrewd investor, well-versed in the unwritten rules of the business world.

The Serpent Parent

Serpents make responsible parents, devoting much time and effort to secure their children's future. They are exceptionally keen to see their children do well at school or in college. The child of a Serpent parent is often an academic achiever. They enjoy considerable parental support and encouragement from a very early age. Both Serpent mothers and fathers are happy to teach their infants to read and write, while older children will benefit from the Serpent's help with homework. Serpent parents spare no expense in stocking the home with books, learning-aids and educational toys. They are prepared to spend their hard-earned money to ensure that their children get the very best start in life.

The Serpent Child

Serpents are studious children. They often devote more time to learning than they do to play. Indeed, they may need open encouragement to mix with other children. Many Serpent children actually prefer adult company. They mature early and are capable of standing their ground in most situations.

Unlike many young people, the Serpent child is particularly good with finances. Pocket money is unlikely to be blown at the first opportunity on chocolates and candy, but saved toward something more important such as holidays or Christmas presents. Like their adult counterparts, the Serpent child is seldom wasteful and has a thrifty attitude toward life in general.

The Serpent Friend

Although the Serpent is a sign of confidence, many born in this cycle are wary of casual acquaintances. The Serpent is cautious by nature and others may need to prove themselves worthy of their trust. Furthermore, Serpents expect much in return for their friendship. They expect to share and share alike with their friends, and hate to feel excluded from any area of their lives.

Although Serpents are dedicated workers, they also know how to have a good time. They will often devote themselves as much to entertainment as they do to work – an evening out is expected to be a fun-filled excursion. During social occasions the one thing the Serpent just cannot abide is someone talking shop. Anyone who continues an office conversation or brings up the subject of work is likely to find themselves immediately cut short by an irate Serpent. Although they will readily enjoy themselves, Serpents do not seek to be the centre of attention. The Serpent may be self-assured but they are also self-conscious. Few Serpents are prepared to make a fool of themselves on the dance floor or to get drunk and lose control.

The Serpent Partner

Serpents are seldom eager to show their feelings. They need to trust someone completely before sharing their true emotions. Consequently, the Serpent partner may need to make all the first moves. Although witty in conversation, Serpents are frequently shy with the opposite sex, finding it difficult to initiate a conversation with someone they find attractive. As women are not usually expected to make the first move, this is less of a problem for the Serpent female. For the Serpent male, however, it can sometimes hinder his love life. So often a girl will fail to realize that the Serpent man is actually interested in her.

Serpents are sensitive and committed lovers, but break-ups are exceptionally difficult for them to handle. They hate the thought that they may have given so much of themselves only to be rejected. On the outside they seem to cope, but inside they may be devastated. A failed relationship can create an especially cynical Serpent. Few Serpents continue to chase or seek the attentions of an ex-partner – they have too much pride. The chief problem is for their next relationship. They may be suspicious of the true intentions of their future partner, or restrained in the commitments they themselves are prepared to make. It can be some time before the Serpent has recovered sufficiently to again abandon emotional inhibitions.

Affinity Signs

The Hero: Serpents are creative concerning practical endeavours, while the Hero is a sign of practical application. Consequently, the two signs compliment one another. Both signs also lead similar social lives and close friendships and attachments are common.

Etana: Although Serpents and Etanas are opposites in many respects, their traits and attributes are complimentary. The Serpent is patient and plans long and hard; the Etana is impetuous. The Serpent can restrain the Etana, while the Etana can bring more spontaneity to the Serpent's life.

The Sphinx: The wise Serpent and the cunning Sphinx usually share a common outlook on life and enjoy many of the same interests. Mutual respect, affection and compatibility is often found between these two signs.

The Huntress: The Serpent love of learning is much respected by the Huntress. The Serpent finds the Huntress' unique insight equally fascinating. The two signs work well together and marriages are often successful.

Problem Signs

The Oryx: The Serpent is generally a sign where the Oryx finds greatest difficulty. Serpents enjoy taking charge too much for the Oryx's liking.

The Phoenix: Those born in the sign of the Phoenix find it difficult to cope with the leadership qualities of the Serpent. Serpents sometimes find Phoenixes too inconsistent in their behaviour.

The Serpent: As many Serpents are somewhat reserved by nature, and unwilling to reveal their inner feelings, two Serpents together tend to be overcautious in their attitudes to one another.

Other Signs

Cascaya: Serpents and Cascayans mix well enough, although close relationships are rare. Serpents are too pragmatic and take life too seriously for the Cascayan. Many Serpents consider Cascayans to be irresponsible.

Assari: Assaris find the Serpent's love of learning of

considerable interest. However, they may distrust the Serpent's laid-back approach to life.

The Genie: These two signs can share close friendships. Romantic relationships may be hampered due to the Serpent's inquisitiveness, which the Genie often finds disconcerting.

The Swallow: Swallows and Serpents share little in common. However, this can sometimes lead to successful marriages. There is little for them to argue or disagree about.

The Griffin: Griffins like to know precisely where they stand with others and most find the Serpent difficult to fathom.

The Dragon: Many Serpents feel that Dragons reveal too much about themselves and some may regard this as a weakness. Dragons, for their part, may consider that Serpents lead a far too conventional life-style.

Famous Serpents

Hillary Clinton. Born: 26 October 1947.

Cool, controlled and calculating, Hillary Clinton has all the Serpent traits of cunning. The Serpent will often formulate a plan and spend years waiting patiently for the right moment to act. Hard work and determination, coupled with the Serpent virtue of patience, has made Hillary Clinton into both a successful career woman in her own right and a powerful aid in her husband's progress. Eloquent and erudite, Hillary has the enviable Serpent capacity to convince others of her ideas and, like the Serpent, her timing is spot on: she can strike at just the right time. Observant, and with a keen eye for detail, the Serpent seldom misses a trick. Hillary Clinton is always quick to assert her authority in a decisive Serpent manner.

Carl Sagan. Born: 9 November 1934.

Since ancient times the Serpent has been a symbol of wisdom and knowledge. Typifying this primary Serpent attribute is the internationally renowned cosmologist and astronomer Carl Sagan. As a leading authority on the mysteries of space, time and the origins of the universe, he displays all the Serpent traits of intellectual curiosity. Those born in this cycle are often inquisitive, and unsolved riddles are always an eagerly accepted challenge. Dr Sagan has devoted his life to exploring the greatest mysteries of all. Serpents make excellent teachers, and Carl Sagan's published and broadcast works have opened up the wonders of the universe to young and old the world over.

Tina Turner. Born: 26 November 1939.

Whatever she has turned her talents to, singer or actress, Tina Turner has introduced her own powerful approach. She may sometimes be difficult to work with, but when allowed to do things her way the outcome is usually successful. Serpents have the enviable ability to sense when something is going to work. Often it is more a matter of firm practical sense rather than any kind of intuition. Tina is very much an individual, and like most born in this cycle she is not prepared to blindly follow trends or fashions. Instead, she has created her own personal style which others have attempted to mimic.

Fate and Fortune

Over the course of the year Serpents can expect the following influences to affect their lives during the separate lunar cycles:

Cascaya: The month of Cascaya can bring to fruition a Serpent plan. It is also the time of year when new opportunities arise. It is an especially good period for a move of job or location should either be sought.

The Phoenix: The usual success of the Serpent's quick-fire response can be upset during the month of the Phoenix. In legend the Phoenix burned to ashes; opportunities can go up in smoke for a Serpent during this cycle.

The Hero: The Hero is a positive sign for the Serpent. This is a favourable month for relationships to flourish. Success is especially likely for the Serpent on the look-out for a new partner.

Assari: The Serpent is a creature of the earth and Assari, although a flying beast, is agile and nimble-footed on solid ground. The two signs work well together, and the Serpent will find that others will see things their way. This is a particularly favourable month for sport and leisure activities. Any Serpent involved in competition is likely to be rewarded with much success.

The Genie: In the month of the Genie financial matters and business affairs are well-placed. This is also a romantic month for the Serpent.

The Griffin: Serpents are inquisitive and like to know

exactly what is going on around them. The multifarious Griffin can cloud the Serpent's vision – there may be too much happening for Serpents to see in all directions. They should avoid being suspicious of situations of which they are not fully informed.

The Oryx: The month of the Oryx can be full of surprise for the Serpent. This is also an excellent time for a vacation.

Etana: Etana acts as the message bearer for the Serpent. Serpents can expect favourable news during this month.

The Serpent: Serpents work remarkably well during their own month. For Serpents involved in academic pursuits, this is a month of much reward. Serpents in business also fare particularly well during this cycle. In domestic life positive news concerning financial affairs can be expected.

The Dragon: As the Dragon and the Serpent are similar creatures there could be conflicts of interest during this month. Particularly in relationships, the Serpent should avoid disputes. The working Serpent should also be careful of disagreements in the factory or office – matters may not work out the way they intended.

The Sphinx: The wise Serpent has little difficulty solving the Sphinx's eternal riddle. A long-standing enterprise may come to fruition. This is a time especially favourable for new relationships, romance and love. It is also a lucky month for anything connected with chance.

The Swallow: The Swallow is a bird seldom seen to

land, while the Serpent lives its life on the ground. The two signs accordingly have little influence upon one another. This can be a time of inactivity, even boredom, for the Serpent.

The Huntress: During the rare Huntress month the Serpent could find that events are completely beyond their control. Unexpected circumstances may arise to alter the course of the Serpent's life.

THE DRAGON

Approximate Calendar Month
DECEMBER

Sign Chart Letter
J

THE DRAGON

THE fire-breathing Dragon is perhaps the most feared of all legendary beasts, yet it is seen as a symbol of mystical power throughout the world. Others may feel vulnerable in the presence of those born in this sign; nevertheless, many seek their guidance and leadership. Dragons, however, are reluctant leaders, usually preferring to go it alone. Blessed with an abundance of mental energy, they are capable of handling most tasks that befall them. Natural creatures of fire, Dragons have the enviable capacity not to get burned; after a crisis they usually land firmly on their feet.

Dragons possess intellectual vitality, mental dexterity and a lively imagination. The Dragon is one of the most eloquent of signs and many Dragons can argue an opponent until blue in the face. Those born in this cycle have endless optimism for their chosen pursuits. Forever formulating plans and new ideas, Dragons can sometimes be tiring, even draining, on friends and acquaintances.

Not only are Dragons blessed with boundless faith and optimism, they are also endowed with vision and foresight. They have a deep sense of intuition and seem to know precisely what others are thinking and planning. An alert mind enables Dragons to determine the full potential of opportunities, and few take long to reach decisions. Impulsiveness sometimes stems from this love of action, and there is a tendency for Dragons to rush headlong into ventures much too readily. Dragons are highly active and many born in this sign excel in sport and games.

Positive Characteristics

An energetic personality guarantees Dragons success in most undertakings. Extremely versatile, they can turn their hands to many varied endeavours. Mentally agile and quick to learn, the majority of those born in this cycle are observant and have a remarkably good memory. They possess artistic talents, especially concerning writing and music, and express themselves in a popular, dramatic fashion. With an exceptional ability to cope in times of difficulty, Dragons are optimistic and enthusiastic about whatever they are doing.

Negative Characteristics

Dragons are unwilling to change their opinions even when proved wrong. They are impatient, jump to conclusions far too quickly, and are apt to make errors of judgement based on hasty decisions or first impressions. Many born in this sign have a quarrelsome temperament, often disagreeing for the sheer sake of it. When they want to, however, the Dragon can charm and flatter anyone into agreement; they just love discussion, debate and argument.

Appearance

Dragons are energetic and restless, finding it difficult to sit quietly for any length of time. They need to be constantly occupied, many being slim or even skinny as a consequence of the nervous energy they expend. Many born in this sign have expressive faces, with a rigidly defined bone structure and quick-fire or penetrating eyes.

Health

Dragons are remarkably resilient to viral infections, usually immune to the coughs and colds to which others annually succumb. They seldom get headaches, stomach bugs or any of the common complaints that plague the modern world. When the Dragon does fall ill – which is rarely – it is generally with something exotic or unusual. The only drawback to the Dragon's robust constitution is their need for abundant sleep. Some signs can survive on next to no rest at all; deprived of their eight or more hours, Dragons will virtually cease to function. At best, the tired Dragon will be irritable, grumpy and unable to concentrate.

The Formula for Success

Dragons work remarkably well in short, sharp bursts. They apply themselves with speed and determination to whatever they are doing. They have a multiplicity of talents, both creative and practical. With an astute memory and inquiring mind, those born in this sign are especially clever at arguing a point. They can skilfully sidetrack an opponent and have them tied up with their own words. Many Dragons are highly intelligent and able to grasp the most complex of problems. They excel at solving conundrums or riddles of any kind. Dragons are exceptionally optimistic and refuse to concede defeat under any circumstance. They make quick decisions and act decisively.

Words of Advice

In excess, the Dragon's positive attributes become their negative traits. Their optimistic streak is a considerable drawback if something is an obvious failure. Their blanket refusal to concede defeat will sometimes tie the Dragon to a doomed endeavour, preventing them from applying themselves to anything fresh. Their displays of boundless enthusiasm can also be misleading to others. Acquaintances may be captivated by a Dragon's idea, only to discover that the Dragon's interest was only skin deep. Dragons should try to moderate their behaviour. It is not that they are deceitful, they simply have tunnel vision.

Suitable Occupations

Dragons are suited for occupations involving quick reactions or calculations. They also excel in work which necessitates close customer contact. They have a lively personality with a friendly and enthusiastic countenance. Many lecturers and teachers are born in this sign, as are writers and broadcasters. Journalism and other investigative work also have strong appeal to Dragons. Their mental dexterity, often coupled with a devotion to physical fitness, means that many professional athletes and successful sportspeople are born in this sign.

The Dragon at Work

Dragons value their freedom above all else. They hate being restricted or compromised in any situation. For this reason they are best suited to occupations which allow them freedom of movement, and the scope to make decisions and handle matters in their own fashion. Dragons aim to reach the very pinnacle of whatever profession they choose. Even when not in a position of power they need the authority to use their own initiative. They are generally popular with colleagues, although they may sometimes disturb those with whom they work closely. Dragons have a tendency to adopt a loud or flamboyant working style.

Dragons like to see a project though from start to finish. They are unhappy joining any enterprise which is already well under way. If they are not involved from the outset, fully informed of every detail, they feel excluded and attempt to change the established procedure. This can result in conflict with those in authority and create friction with peers. The Dragon's roar is worse than its bite, however. Few Dragons are aggressive or vindictive by nature; a good argument usually clears the air for most born in this sign.

The Dragon Woman

The Dragon woman has an aura of self-confidence and a glowing personality. Unlike Dragon men who sometimes keep their fiery temperament hidden beneath a cool exterior, the Dragon woman will often display her vitality to full advantage. She is every bit a lady, however, even though she may be something of a tomboy in her youth. Many women born in this sign are keen on physical fitness, and most can hold their ground in male company.

The Dragon is not the tidiest of women, quite content in jeans, an old sweater or a track suit when at home. It is a different matter when she is at work or attending a special engagement; then she will dress to impress. The Dragon career woman will appear neat and efficient, whereas the Dragon woman at a social occasion will dress in a particularly feminine style. She will always look the part in whatever she is doing.

A great lover of animals, the Dragon woman is likely to own many pets. Even if her circumstances only permit her a single cat or dog, it will be treated almost as one of the family.

The Dragon Man

The male of this sign is often a born performer. Not only is he an excellent entertainer, at ease in most circumstances, he will adapt his style and humour to suit the occasion. The Dragon man loves to surround his life with excitement, even mystery. Unlike some signs who may find it necessary to create an enigmatic aura to hide a lack of self-confidence, the Dragon just loves to fascinate those around him. The Dragon man is a boy at heart; always eager to be the centre of attention, he is the soul of any party.

Most Dragon men are attracted to dominant women. Indeed, an assertive partner is often essential for the Dragon man. He is one of the laziest and most untidy of men when it comes to household or domestic matters, needing someone who is prepared to handle this side of his life. If he does marry a more subservient woman the home environment is likely to end up a right old mess.

The Dragon Parent

Dragons encourage their children to do well, although they will seldom push them too hard. They usually manage to inspire their children through sheer enthusiasm. Dragons have the marvellous ability to make life interesting, and learning is a fascinating and exciting experience for children of a Dragon mother or father. Both are always ready to take time from whatever they are doing – no matter how important – to help and advise their young. Dragons run a happy, but not a particularly tidy home. They are ready to go to any lengths to prepare their children for working life, but neatness and orderly habits are something their offspring will need to learn elsewhere.

The Dragon Child

Dragons are some of the most hyperactive children. They demand much attention and need many outlets for their energy. They mix well with others, young and old alike, but have a tendency to monopolize everyone in their vicinity. They may be gifted artistically, academically or mechanically, but the ability to apply themselves to school or college work is often lacking. They are just too easily distracted. Their intelligence and capacity to rapidly assimilate information provides many born in this sign with the potential to be top of the class – if only they concentrate a little more.

The Dragon Friend

Dragons share a marvellous, sometimes zany sense of humour. They always have the right joke or pertinent remark for any occasion. They are hospitable and friendly, and although Dragons need to be constantly occupied, their friends will seldom be bored in their company.

Dragons are not particularly keen on the more conservative forms of entertainment. Sitting quietly for hours at the opera, theatre or cinema is unlikely to appeal to many born in the Dragon sign. They prefer to be actively entertained, if not personally involved. Both the men and women of this sign are fond of music, and disco-dancing or loud rock concerts are especially enjoyed by younger Dragons.

Dragons intend to live life to the full and usually expect others to do likewise. If a friend prefers a more serene life-style, they are unlikely to get much peace with the Dragon around. Dragons like to keep in touch with distant friends, but their circle of acquaintances is often so large that it may be sometime before they finally get around to contacting each in turn.

One annoying habit which is almost the Dragon's hallmark is the tendency to take far too long getting ready to go out. 'I'll just be a minute,' the Dragon will promise, and an hour later you're still waiting. Regardless of excuses, the Dragon is hopeless when it comes to estimating how long anything is going to take.

The Dragon Partner

Few Dragons will happily spend time alone. They need company to be truly content. Consequently, Dragons will seldom be without a partner for long. Many marry early, and those who don't will spend as much time as possible with their partner. They are not domineering or possessive, they just need someone around to give them encouragement and much-needed companionship.

Both men and women of this sign are passionate and uninhibited lovers, and give themselves fully to any romance. A love of variety and adventure makes Dragons exciting and stimulating partners. Although both Dragon men and women are often excessive in their chosen pursuits, they are usually careful with their money. A girl expecting endless gifts or an expensive night out from her Dragon man is in for disappointment. A man hoping to go Dutch and share the cost of a date with his Dragon girl is also in for a shock. Dragons are not averse to luxury, they just refuse to spend their hard-earned money in an extravagant or unnecessary way.

Affinity Signs

The Hero: The industrious and optimistic Dragon is admired by the Hero. Both signs share the ability to consistently devote themselves to a single goal or objective.

The Sphinx: The Sphinx is often cool and relaxed in most situations. The hyperactive Dragon seldom disturbs the Sphinx, while the Sphinx's cunning and lively intelligence is much appreciated by the Dragon. These two signs compliment each other nicely, although it may seem to others that Sphinxes and Dragons are worlds apart.

The Dragon: Most Dragons enjoy the company of others like themselves. Although they will often be messy or untidy together, they make excellent close friends and partners, sharing a love of excitement and adventure.

The Huntress: Huntresses can take the energetic Dragon in their stride. Dragons often need a benevolent and controlling hand which the Huntress is prepared to offer. Almost all the attributes lacking in one sign are compensated by the other, and some of the most successful marriages are formed between Huntresses and Dragons.

Problem Signs

The Genie: Genii and Dragons often clash. The overactive Dragon is just too disquieting for the Genie's peace of mind.

Etana: The energetic Dragon and the flighty Etana will often argue and bicker even when they see eye-to-eye.

The Griffin: Dragons and Griffins share similar creativity. However, the headstrong Griffin can often clash with the fiery temperament of the Dragon. Neither is prepared to give way to the other.

The Swallow: The Dragon's energetic mental agility is fascinating, though exhausting, to the peace-loving Swallow.

Other Signs

Cascaya: Dragons like to commit themselves to long-term relationships. The Cascayan is quickly irritated by anything which becomes routine or lacks variety.

The Phoenix: Both the Dragon and the Phoenix are signs of extreme optimisim, and the two get on like a house on fire – after all, they are both creatures of fire. Unfortunately, the restraining element of other signs is needed by both. When alone together the Phoenix and the Dragon can find themselves in adverse situations which are difficult to remedy.

The Oryx: The Dragon's optimism and will to succeed is admired by Oryxes, although they may become frustrated by the Dragon's failure to see the obvious.

Assari: Relationships between Assaris and Dragons are particularly volatile. They may adore one another, sharing a love of adventure, travel and excitement. When together, however, both can find their emotions too readily stimulated and arguments may ensue. These signs often share a love-hate relationship.

The Serpent: Many Serpents feel that Dragons reveal too much about themselves, and some may regard this as a weakness. Dragons, for their part, may consider that Serpents lead far too conventional a life-style.

Famous Dragons

Uri Geller. Born: 20 December 1946.

The Dragon has long been a symbol of magic and mystery. Who better to typify the mystical Dragon than the mysterious Uri Geller? Dragons are often natural performers, not only possessing the ability to entertain but to positively respond to audience reaction. Like many Dragons Uri Geller knows precisely how to popularize his unusual talents. Dragons are problem solvers and fast thinkers, and Uri's alert mind and mental dexterity is typical of the quick-thinking Dragon. The adult Dragon is often a youngster at heart, and typically Uri Geller exudes a youthful enthusiasm which his audience finds captivating.

Anthony Hopkins. Born: 31 December 1937.

Actor Anthony Hopkins is typical of the male Dragon, having a fiery heart wrapped within a cool exterior. Outwardly calm, almost serene, he hides his energetic temperament and powerful determination behind composed and calculating eyes. Like many Dragons, Anthony is an incredibly versatile performer, able to turn his talents to whatever is required. The Dragon is a natural creature of fire and fiercely independent in approach to most endeavours. This prime Dragon trait has afforded Anthony Hopkins the freedom to achieve his ambitions in a unique and individual fashion.

Jane Fonda. Born: 21 December 1937.

The queen of physical fitness, Jane Fonda has combined her acting talents and business acumen to become a highly successful woman in many walks of life. She exudes an aura of self-assuredness and a glowing vitality which is typical of the Dragon sign. Like many Dragon women she displays a fiery passion in all her ventures. Many born in the Dragon sign can accomplish the most dramatic changes of role or career. It is not surprising, therefore, that Jane Fonda, once one of the world's most sought-after sex symbols, later became a major figure in the Women's Movement.

Fate and Fortune

Over the course of the year Dragons can expect the following influences to affect their lives during the separate lunar cycles:

Cascaya: The cool, fast-flowing waters of the Cascayan month may quench the Dragon's fire. Dragons should be careful during this time not to argue or strongly disagree with those around them. If they do, they may find themselves embarrasingly defeated.

The Phoenix: Both the Phoenix and the Dragon are fire signs in the extreme. During this month the Dragon imagination will be at its most inventive. New projects are likely to succeed due to quick reactions. Romance is especially favoured, and new and exciting relationships are likely to be formed.

The Hero: Few Dragons will find a Hero month a time of peace or tranquillity. Domestic circumstances may require much of the Dragon's attention. If Dragons make certain to divide their time equally between work, rest and play this month should pass quite favourably.

Assari: At no other time of the year is the Dragon more likely to lose patience than during the month of Assari.

Problems in relationships with close friends or relatives may occur as a result of Dragon irritability.

The Genie: Travel and change of work or location is favoured during the month of the Genie. If the Dragon intends to move house this can be a particularly advantageous time to begin the process. Similarly, if they are considering a change of job they should profit by looking for new work at this time.

The Griffin: For the Dragon, the artful Griffin brings a month of inspiration. Now, more than at any other time of the year, is the Dragon likely to benefit from sound and fruitful ideas. This is an especially promising month for love, romance and affairs of the heart.

The Oryx: The month of the Oryx is a cycle of much activity for Dragons, but they should be careful not to overwork. The Dragon may become touchy or sensitive concerning the opinions of others. It is, however, an extremely favourable time for sport and other leisure activities.

Etana: Anything concerning group activities, either social or business in nature, is well-placed for the Dragon. Any Dragon who takes the lead at this time of the year is likely to find themselves in a fortuitous or profitable situation.

The Serpent: The Dragon and the Serpent are similar creatures and, as such, there could be conflicts of interest during this month. Particularly concerning relationships, the Dragon should be careful of involving themselves in disputes – they will probably end up worse off.

The Dragon: During their own month many Dragons find excitement and adventure, particularly in romance and love. The Dragon is an especially active creature and should take care not to work too hard during this period.

The Sphinx: The Sphinx is the message-bearer for the Dragon, and unusual news may arrive in the earlier days of this cycle. The Dragon is still well-placed for romance during the month of the Sphinx, while new acquaintances – particularly connected with financial matters – are very much on the cards.

The Swallow: The Swallow is a swift and graceful bird, while the Dragon is a strong and powerful beast. The Dragon may accordingly overwhelm any subtle influence that the Swallow month may bring. During this cycle Dragons should be particularly attentive to the smaller details of life, lest they overlook important, sometimes obvious possibilities.

The Huntress: The month of the Huntress is a time when Dragons are exceptionally lucky. They should be careful, however, not to overplay their hand. If they know when to call it a day, the Huntress month can bring fulfilment in nearly every aspect of the Dragon's life.

THE SPHINX

Approximate Calendar Month
JANUARY

Sign Chart Letter
K

THE SPHINX

THIS is probably the most enigmatic of all the signs. In Babylonian legend the Sphinx was not only a treasure guardian but also a shape-shifter: a metamorphose entity able to change into the form of any other creature. Similarly, those born in the cycle of the Sphinx share many characteristics with other signs. They have the physical attributes of the Griffin and the Hero, the innovative power of the Phoenix, and mental agility of the Serpent. The Sphinx woman is similar to the Assari woman, while the Sphinx man is similar to the Dragon. As children they are like little Heroes, but as parents they share many Dragon child-rearing characteristics. Most of all, Sphinxes can modify and adapt their behaviour to suit their present company and current predicament.

In legend the Sphinx set a riddle to be solved before its secrets would be revealed. Those born in this cycle are forever challenging the world around them; not in an antagonistic manner, but certainly with a gleam in their eyes. They possess a mischievous quality which sometimes bewilders those around them, and few but the most vigilant will know the Sphinx's true intentions.

The Sphinx was also a sign of mystical power, and another remarkable Sphinx trait is uncanny foresight.

More often than not, circumstances will unfold just the way the Sphinx predicted. This unusual ability is due to a deep sense of intuition; an instinctive awareness which would make the Sphinx an excellent detective.

Positive Characteristics

Outwardly the Sphinx is humorous, witty and fun-loving, but inwardly they maintain a serious, sharp-eyed attitude to life. They are ambitious, with the capacity to exercise authority, while a strong will and conscientious attitude results in many Sphinxes holding positions of responsibility. Sphinxes are always optimistic concerning their chosen ventures and a strong sense of intuition often brings them much success. They have considerable powers of concentration, coupled with manifold technical and artistic skills. Those born in this cycle are also extremely self-disciplined, possessing the mental stamina to remain on top of most situations.

Negative Characteristics

Opportunities are sometimes missed through too great an attachment to outdated ideas or methods. Sphinxes tend to make errors of judgement based on strongly-held opinions. Moreover, many born in this sign share unrealistic expectations, and so disappointments are bound to arise. Others may consider Sphinxes to be arrogant or vain at times. They may also find Sphinx intuition disturbing. Additionally, Sphinxes are frequently too inquisitive for their own good. In times of difficulty there is also a marked tendency for Sphinxes to blame others for problems of their own making.

Appearance

The Sphinx shares physical characteristics with the Griffin and the Hero. Like the Hero, they have firm features and a confident and authoritative stature. The Sphinx usually has a benevolent gaze and exudes an aura of self-assuredness. Like the Griffin, they move with an air of certainty, they carry their heads high and walk with their backs straight. Few are quick or erratic, most being slow and deliberate movers.

Health

In health Sphinxes again share Griffin and Hero traits. Like the Hero, the Sphinx is a physically active cycle, and so injuries and broken limbs are more common than for other signs. Like Griffins, few Sphinxes are worriers and are seldom concerned about their own well-being. Many are inclined to ignore preventative medicine or disregard any tell-tale signs of illness. Repetitive strain injuries, or other such ailments which are best tackled early, may be left unattended. Similar to the Griffin, this can lead to complications which might easily have been avoided.

The Formula for Success

The Sphinx's formula for success appears to be comprised of elements from the Phoenix and the Serpent signs. Like the Phoenix, Sphinxes are always eager for new experiences and ready to rise to any challenge. Unlike the Phoenix, however, they do not endeavour to fill their days with such excitement that they forget about the more practical matters of life. Sphinxes will keep a watchful eye on every detail of their ventures. They can create opportunities from very little and are one of the most enterprising of all the signs.

With the Serpent they share attributes of objectivity,

refusing to judge a book by its cover. They seldom, if ever, jump to conclusions about anything, and refuse to allow prejudice to cloud their judgement. They have patience concerning most endeavours and accurately gauge the correct moment to act. They also have the capacity to grasp the root of a problem, possessing shrewd insight into the true cause of difficulties they encounter. Like the Serpent, Sphinxes are forthright and astute, they have inquiring and probing minds and are remarkably self-disciplined.

Words of Advice

Sphinxes can be far too cynical at times, refusing to believe anything which has not been seen with their own eyes. They are unlikely to take anything at face value or on someone else's word. Again like Serpents, Sphinxes should try to have a little more faith in human nature. Sphinxes also feel impelled to know the detailed affairs of those around them, and are sometimes too inquisitive for their own good. By contrast, few Sphinxes will reveal their own motivations or intentions. Sphinxes should learn to give and take a little more, particularly in business or professional matters.

Suitable Occupations

Whether as a manual or white-collar worker, the Sphinx is generally most successful when self-employed. Sphinxes make especially good entrepreneurs, managers or supervisors. They watch and listen carefully before arriving at conclusions, and only do so after every angle has been considered. Accordingly, they make solid judgements and usually take sound commercial decisions. Furthermore, they are quick to assert authority in a firm, decisive manner. Because of their multifarious attributes, Sphinxes are found in just about any occupation, and can easily change horses in mid-stream should the need arise.

The Sphinx at Work

Success is assured in any business matter providing colleagues are prepared to let Sphinxes do things their own way. Sphinxes make tough but fair employers, although they may drive their employees a little too hard. They are equally hard on themselves, however, and use their many talents with remarkable dedication. They have the enviable quality of being able to concentrate fully on whatever they are doing, and can always be trusted to do any job to the best of their ability. Again they share common traits with the Serpent, finding it difficult to socialize with close business associates. Many Sphinxes keep their working lives quite separate from their social lives.

The Sphinx Woman

The Sphinx woman is almost identical to the Assari woman. She is a great conversationalist and an eager listener. Many men are enchanted by her eloquent manner and flamboyant personality. She has an enigmatic demeanour which allows her to stand out from the crowd. The Sphinx woman enjoys much attention and, like the Assari, she may be the object of jealousy.

Most women born in the cycle of the Sphinx are neat and tidy, although they are more concerned with personal appearance than domestic order. Like the Assari, the Sphinx woman usually spends so much time concentrating on her hair, clothes and make-up, that housework is often left unattended. The Sphinx woman does not dress like the Assari, however. In this respect she is more like the Hero, certain to be wearing the latest middle-of-the-road style, but nothing outrageous or unusual.

The Sphinx woman will take a central role in social activities, and in business makes one of the most successful career women. She is always ready to give advice and is prepared to offer comfort to those in distress. She keeps her own problems to herself, however. Outwardly, she may seem unemotional and, unless angered, she will keep her true feelings very much to herself.

The Sphinx Man

The male of this sign is very similar to the Dragon: a born performer, an excellent entertainer and at ease in most company. He loves to surround his life with excitement, and can adapt his character and humour to suit the occasion. The Sphinx will fascinate those around him and is always prepared to be the centre of attention.

Sphinx men will divide their time equally between business affairs and leisure activities. They can be somewhat ruthless in commercial dealings. Like the Dragon, the Sphinx man expects his competitors and rivals to be as hardened as he. However, when all is said and done, the Sphinx is a sociable animal and loves to make everything as enjoyable as possible.

Sphinx men are sparing with their deepest affections and expect others to share their sentiments before they are prepared to commit themselves to long-lasting friendships or relationships. To all those who share their life, the Sphinx is a fascinating acquaintance. Not only are Sphinxes well-read and knowledgeable on many subjects, they will discuss anything in an enlightening and entertaining manner.

The Sphinx Parent

Sphinx parents are very similar to Griffin parents in the way they bring up their young. Although caring, they are inclined to treat their family like an efficient business concern. Like the Griffin, Sphinx fathers have a tendency to act like firm but fair employers, while Sphinx mothers are especially concerned about their children's appearance. Both will ensure that their children are well looked after, but they tend to neglect their emotional needs. Instead they concentrate on the child's outer physical welfare, such as health, appearance, good manners and practical achievements. Like the Griffin, Sphinxes can be benevolent and affectionate, merely wanting the very best for their young.

The Sphinx Child

As youngsters Sphinxes behave like Hero children. Right from infancy they will be responsive to education and eager to learn. Sphinx children are inquisitive in the extreme, wanting to know the reason for everything. They work diligently at school and usually do well in class. There are seldom bad reports of the Sphinx child's academic achievements and most also do well in sport. Many children of this sign are born competitors.

The Sphinx child has a constructive attitude to life, and few born in this cycle are likely to be rude, unkind or destructive in any way. They mix well with other children and are polite to adults, though many need constant attention and praise for their achievements. Their leadership qualities develop early; the young Sphinx will often insist on taking the lead with friends.

The Sphinx Friend

Usually the Sphinx will read a situation perfectly. They often have tremendous insight into what is both appealing and popular, and can captivate their friends with original and imaginative ideas. The Sphinx is not only a sign of creativity, it is also a sign of communication; many born in this cycle make the most entertaining hosts and companions.

Sphinxes have versatility of character and can adapt themselves to most company. Innate performing skills are a usual Sphinx trait, and many born in this sign can assume tailor-made personalities to fit readily into whatever circumstances surround them. The Sphinx has a firm sense of loyalty, and the close bond which they often share with their families must be accepted by friends and lovers alike.

The Sphinx Partner

The Sphinx is a sign of insight and most born in this cycle know precisely the right way to treat a prospective partner. They can readily adapt themselves to saying what others hope to hear, and will act to impress. There is nothing false about this remarkable Sphinx versatility. Sphinxes simply enjoy fitting in with others and with the spirit of an occasion.

Sphinxes have silver tongues, and Sphinx praise and flattery is hard to ignore. Romantics will find themselves captivated by the magnetic personality of the extrovert, self-assured Sphinx. They can adapt their interests and outlooks on life to suit their lover, and are often the most accommodating of partners. Sphinxes so hate discord in their domestic lives that they will go to tremendous lengths to avoid matrimonial squabbles or lovers' tiffs. Unless an argument concerns something about which they feel strongly, Sphinxes much prefer to concede defeat for the sake of peace.

Sphinxes have a mysterious, enigmatic quality which others either love or fear. The Sphinx is usually so good at whatever they turn their minds to that they can be somewhat arrogant at times. This is seldom hollow vanity; rather an assured confidence which may be misconstrued. Like the enigmatic side of their nature, Sphinx assuredness is either distrusted or admired.

Affinity Signs

The Hero: The Sphinx is the sign which the Hero often admires the most. Their ability to make something out of nothing, together with their keen financial instinct, are greatly respected by the Hero. It is usually impossible for the Sphinx to ignore Hero flattery.

The Serpent: The wise Serpent and the cunning Sphinx usually share a common outlook on life and enjoy many of the same interests. Mutual respect, affection and compatibility is often found between these two signs.

The Dragon: The Sphinx is cool and relaxed in most situations. The hyperactive Dragon seldom disturbs the Sphinx, while the Sphinx's cunning and lively intelligence is much appreciated by the Dragon. These two signs compliment each other nicely, although it may seem to others that Sphinxes and Dragons are worlds apart.

The Swallow: The openness of the Swallow is appreciated by the Sphinx, while the Swallow is captivated by Sphinx inscrutability. Successful relationships and marriages are highly probable.

Etana: Etanas and Sphinxes often mix well. The Sphinx

has many ideas which they lack the courage to try. The Etana is quite prepared to implement the Sphinx's schemes. These signs often make ideal partners in marriage.

Problem Signs

The Oryx: The Sphinx is the sign that the Oryx finds hardest to fathom. Their ability to make something out of nothing, and their keen financial sense, are mysteries to the Oryx.

The Griffin: In legend both the Griffin and the Sphinx were treasure guardians. Those born in these signs often experience a clash of interests and personality. Sometimes they may even distrust one another.

Cascaya: The meticulous Sphinx can be most annoying to the Cascayan. The two signs have markedly different temperaments and little in common.

Other Signs

The Phoenix: The Phoenix dislike of financial matters is well compensated by the Sphinx. The Sphinx is both conservative and thrifty in approach to most endeavours, and the Phoenix respects such attributes in others.

The Genie: The Genie loves a mystery and the Sphinx's life is often enigmatic. The Genie, however, likes to be treated as an equal and the Sphinx has an arrogant streak which many Genii dislike.

Assari: Assaris generally admire the clever Sphinx, whereas Sphinxes often find the romantic Assari a stimulating companion.

The Sphinx: Two Sphinxes tend to compete with one another, each out to get the upper hand. They are not argumentative by nature, and so this is unlikely to prevent successful, although unusual, relationships.

The Huntress: The Huntress is a sign that can solve the Sphinx's eternal riddle. Huntress intuition gives them the ability to fathom the motives of those born in the cycle of the Sphinx. The Sphinx may find this acutely unnerving.

Famous Sphinxes

Steven Spielberg. Born: 18 December 1947.

Very often Sphinxes will read a situation perfectly. They share tremendous insight into what will be both appealing and popular. Who better to typify this Sphinx trait than top director Steven Spielberg. His movies are always a box-office success, and both young and old alike are captivated by his unique and imaginative creations. The Sphinx is not only a sign of imagination, it is also a sign of communication. All over the world, and at all levels of society, Steven Spielberg's movies communicate to everyone with phenomenal success.

Mel Gibson. Born: 3 January 1956.

Mel Gibson is a typical Sphinx in his versatility of character, which allows him to play so many varied roles. Many Sphinxes are natural actors and Mel handles most of his characters with considerable ease. Performing skills are a usual Sphinx trait, and many born in this sign fit readily into differing situations. Like many Sphinxes, although a good socializer, Mel nevertheless likes to keep his personal life very much apart from his working life. The Sphinx usually has a firm sense of morality and Mel is typical in this respect. Often those born in the sign of the Sphinx have strong family ties, and the close bond which Mel Gibson has with his family is very much a Sphinx characteristic.

Oprah Winfrey. Born: 29 January 1954.

The Sphinx is a sign of insight, and Oprah Winfrey has become the world's best-known chat show host by utilizing this enviable Sphinx trait. She always knows precisely how to handle her guests, either to encourage them to open up or to say exactly what she wants. The Sphinx is also a sign of cunning. To remain on top of a conversation with some of the world's most erudite personalities, Oprah Winfrey has needed every ounce of this useful Sphinx attribute. Few Sphinxes are afraid to exercise authority, and typically Oprah is always in control of her guests and audience alike.

Fate and Fortune

Over the course of the year Sphinxes can expect the following influences to affect their lives during the separate lunar cycles:

Cascaya: During the month of Cascaya all the Sphinx cunning will come into play. It is an especially productive time for business endeavours or matters connected with the professional environment. Promotion at work or recognition for achievement is possible during this month. This is also a month of luck concerning chance endeavours.

The Phoenix: In legend the Sphinx could easily outwit

an opponent ill-prepared to face her. Similarly most born in the Sphinx sign are capable of handling themselves in an argument. The resilient Phoenix, however, can rise majestically from defeat. During this month the Sphinx's usual eloquence may lead them nowhere. It may be a time of considerable stagnation for the Sphinx.

The Hero: In legend the Sphinx was eventually defeated by a questing Hero. This is another month when Sphinx opportunities are somewhat limited. Relationships may suffer if the Sphinx insists on having the upper hand. Business matters may also suffer if Sphinxes remain inflexible in their approach. However, if the Sphinx is prepared to see things from others' points of view, then profitable and rewarding changes of direction may result.

Assari: The nimble Assari brings amusement to the Sphinx. More than any other month this is a time for Sphinxes to let down their hair and enjoy themselves. Sports, games and leisure activities are particularly favoured during this cycle.

The Genie: The Genie month is extremely suited for romance in the Sphinx's life. Existing relationships may take on a fresh and interesting dimension, while new love affairs are possible for the Sphinx who is at present alone.

The Griffin: The Griffin, like the Sphinx, has the body of a lion. The influence of the rampaging lion may be detrimental to the Sphinx during the Griffin month. A headstrong and inflexible approach can cause problems, particularly in domestic affairs. This may be the best month for the Sphinx to take a vacation.

The Oryx: The magical Oryx brings renewal to the Sphinx. Anything which seems to have reached a stalemate can be rejuvenated by the fresh possibilities of this month. If the Sphinx has become bogged down with a problem the solution could present itself toward the end of this cycle. This is an especially favourable month for love, romance and affairs of the heart.

Etana: If a Sphinx is looking for new employment this is a particularly positive time. Similarly, if the Sphinx is thinking of moving home an opportunity to relocate is very possible.

The Serpent: The Serpent acts as the message bearer for the Sphinx, and news from a completely unexpected quarter may be received. The Serpent is a symbol of wisdom, and so the clever Sphinx is particularly astute during this month. Any arguments or disputes are likely to be resolved in the Sphinx's favour.

The Dragon: The Dragon month is a period favourable to any Sphinx involved in sport or other leisure activities, particularly regarding team events. Any team in which the Sphinx plays a major role is likely to triumph.

The Sphinx: The Sphinx is a thinker and often needs time to be alone. This is a month for the Sphinx to plan or merely to contemplate. If the Sphinx keeps a balanced perspective and permits the help of others, solutions to unsolved problems may be discovered.

The Swallow: The Swallow month is a time when Sphinxes find answers where they least expect to find them. The Swallow month is also a time of romance and adventure for the Sphinx.

The Huntress: During a Huntress month the Sphinx will find acquaintances particularly helpful. If Sphinxes abandon their natural suspicion of strangers they will find many new avenues opened up to them.

THE SWALLOW

Approximate Calendar Month
FEBRUARY

Sign Chart Letter
L

THE SWALLOW

SWALLOWS have tremendous creative potential, and once their true vocation is realized success is virtually guaranteed. Often, however, they are too self-conscious of their failures and ignore their achievements. When in difficulty there is also a strong tendency for Swallows to withdraw, occupying themselves with a chosen pursuit which keeps them apart from others. Although graceful in the air, on land the swallow is a vulnerable bird. Similarly, those born in the Swallow sign are more artistic than technical, and materialistic pursuits are best left to others. Just as the swallow is seldom seen to land, a prime trait of those born in this cycle is reticence and hesitation regarding down-to-earth, practical concerns. Their chief obstacle in life is getting started, but once in motion they can achieve remarkable results in no time at all.

Swallows are true romantics and love to fantasize and reminisce. Many share a marvellous talent to captivate an audience, enlivening conversation by their sheer enthusiasm for romance and adventure. The phrase 'still waters run deep' is often an apt description of the Swallow. Indeed, many give the impression that somewhere within their soul there lies a myriad of divine secrets. Swallows are natural performers and a flamboyant, dramatic personality never fails to win friends and gain influence. They enjoy a variety of interests, and few will remain in the same job or social circumstances for their entire lives. Swallows seldom do anything in a conventional style, but lend a showy, theatrical quality to their manifold ventures.

Positive Characteristics

A cheerful temperament makes most relationships easy for Swallows, and many enjoy considerable popularity. Love of social occasions is usual, with much concern for the pleasure and happiness of others. Business capacity is well above average, although partners or colleagues are required to help with sound administration and investments. Most born in this sign have a deep sense of responsibility, generally sharing a conscientious and principled attitude to life. Swallows are dedicated workers who have the ability to devote themselves long and hard to positive effect.

Negative Characteristics

Many Swallows miss vital opportunities due to a hesitant and indecisive attitude. Until proved right or successful, Swallows show a lack of confidence, with too great a dependence on the opinions of others. Extravagance and a love of luxury can create financial problems. Sometimes Swallows have unrealistic ideals or aspirations and disappointments are bound to result. There is the risk that Swallows will withdraw, becoming silent or self-pitying when difficulties arise. There is also a tendency for Swallows to be possessive in relationships.

Appearance

Those born in the sign of the Swallow usually have long and graceful limbs. Endowed with a fine bone structure, the face of the Swallow is warm and sensual.

Their eyes are bright, alert and expressive, often with prominent lashes. Like the swallow bird, they are alert and elegant. Their dress sense can be immaculate, and many Swallows will spend considerable time and effort making certain they look their very best.

Health

The area of the body susceptible to infection is the throat and larynx, and stress-related problems are also common for Swallows. Stiffness of joints is another Swallow complaint, but exercise – so long as it is gentle and regulated – usually relieves discomfort. The Swallow is generally endowed with a sturdy metabolism, though weight problems may result from a fondness for chocolates, cakes and other sweet foods.

The Formula for Success

The helpful Swallow is a valuable member of any group or team, always eager to offer assistance to associates. They bring fresh ideas and their individual approach has panache. Considerate and accommodating, Swallows are prepared to lead by example. Swallows hate discord and will avoid pointless quarrels at all costs. They much prefer to see those around them happy and content, and will go to great lengths to maintain harmony. They will, however, make a firm stand on behalf of friends, arguing their case with eloquence.

Swallows are always ready to accept the valid opinions of others, rarely acting with bias. They possess vivid and colourful imaginations, display much artistic flair and utilize their creative talents toward the common good. Swallows share a close affinity with nature coupled with a highly developed spirituality. They are compassionate and considerate and will try to alleviate suffering wherever it is found.

Words of Advice

The practicalities of life do not always fit well with the Swallow's imaginative aspirations. Many have an unrealistic attitude to material pursuits and frequently suffer disappointment due to high expectations of relationships. Swallows have wonderful humility, and are seldom, if ever, arrogant or vain. Admirable though these qualities are, they may result in too much self-sacrifice and a lack of consideration for their own essential needs. Swallows should make a determined effort not to let acquaintances walk all over them. Those born in this sign are sometimes too kind and generous for their own good.

Suitable Occupations

The caring and understanding Swallow works well with the underprivileged, the sick and the elderly. Their sympathetic nature, coupled with a willingness to listen to the problems of others, make counselling, psychology and social work ideal occupations. Swallows are born communicators and anything entailing persuasion or requiring direct customer contact are also appropriate professions for Swallows. Having an affinity with nature, many Swallows are suited for work involving agriculture, conservation and animal welfare. With a natural flair for the dramatic, many Swallows excel in careers concerning music and drama.

The Swallow at Work

An amiable disposition brings the Swallow popularity in the workplace. Colleagues can safely place their trust in the Swallow; anything told them in confidence is certain to remain a secret. They also provide a sympathetic ear for problems, and offer a firm shoulder on which to cry. Kind as they are, the accommodating

Swallow will not be afraid to speak up on behalf of workmates. They will, however, broach any complaint with considerable diplomacy, refusing to be sidetracked by anger or frustration.

Swallows are diligent and trustworthy workers, capable of intense devotion to duty. They prefer to work in their own way, excelling, so long as they are given ample scope for initiative. They are professionally ambitious, leaving no stone unturned to achieve their objectives. Swallows do not work well under pressure, however, having a tendency to become scatty and forgetful when stressed.

The Swallow Woman

It is important for the Swallow woman to feel good about herself. She will devote much time to her appearance and take great care of her health and fitness. It fills her with horror to think she may not look her best, and will never answer the door to anyone unless she is fully prepared. She even hates her closest friends to visit without warning. The woman of this sign will frequently display an unorthodox attitude towards life, and live according to her own set of rules and values.

The Swallow woman is always prepared to help those in distress. She is gracious and generous, an excellent listener and an amiable friend. She cannot abide gossip, however, refusing to continue with a conversation which turns to criticism of anyone not present. She loves company and is the perfect hostess. Indeed, she feels uneasy when alone, except, that is, when she is getting ready to go out – then she must be allowed to prepare in peace.

The woman of this sign is an elegant dresser. She is not a blind follower of fashion, however, but dresses in a style which suits her. In her opinion, if it does not happen to be the latest trend – so what! She is not the most domesticated of signs but her home will be clean and hygienic. The Swallow woman is one of the most forgetful of any sign, forever mislaying her personal possessions.

The Swallow Man

Like his female counterpart, the Swallow man will not seek to be the centre of attention. If pressed, however, he will rise to any occasion. Swallow men hate inertia; they refuse to be bored under any circumstances and are always searching for new ideas. Once anything becomes routine they look for something else to add to their list of interests. Sometimes they fail to acknowledge their own abilities, lacking faith in their talents and potential.

At home the Swallow man will often start a job, such as painting and decorating or fixing the car, only to leave it unfinished. You can always tell the Swallow man's house by a half-mown lawn or an abandoned piece of home improvement.

The Swallow is a born family man, surrounding his life with love and fellowship. He is one of the most devoted husbands and fathers of any sign, and so long as he has a secure environment to return to each evening he will excel in his chosen profession. He will work confidently with business colleagues, knowing precisely what he wants and how to achieve it. His strength of purpose comes from the knowledge that he is working for the benefit of his family. Indeed, if he were not giving his job his very best he would feel he was letting them down. The Swallow alone is a different matter. The Swallow bachelor, for example, is often the most disorganized of any sign.

The Swallow Parent

Swallows are patient and tolerant parents. They do not believe in punishment or severe reprimand of any kind. Instead, they will let their children make their own mistakes, confident that it is the most valuable way for their offspring to learn. Swallow parents are affectionate and loving and will encourage their young to the full, always giving the very best of advice. Whilst they like their children to be clean and tidy, they are rarely cross if they return home dirty or muddy from play. 'Kids will be kids' is usually the motto of the Swallow parent.

The Swallow Child

The Swallow is a sprightly and inquisitive child. They are also dreamers and often have invisible childhood friends. Indeed, Swallow children will usually talk to themselves more frequently than other signs. That does not mean they do not have real companions; they forge friendships readily and enjoy considerable popularity with other children. They have such a vivid imagination, it is easy for them to create a colourful world of harmless make-believe.

From an early age Swallow children are bright, alert and quick to learn, although they may require encouragement to perform well in school. Provided a subject is presented in a stimulating fashion, however, the Swallow child will take to learning with great enthusiasm. It is up to teachers to make lessons interesting enough for the Swallow to pay attention.

The Swallow Friend

Swallows are special friends, good listeners and entertaining conversationalists, but they must share a common bond or affinity in order to enjoy close friendships. They are easy-going and hate to burden anyone with their own troubles. Swallows refuse to judge their acquaintances, maintaining an open mind in most situations. They only have one failing as friends: they always mean to keep in touch with those who have moved away, but never seem to get around to it. Eventually, having failed to phone or write, they may even feel guilty and contact may sadly be lost for good.

Swallows sometimes seem to exist in an insular, timeless world. They are always late for appointments, hate to be hurried, and insist on doing everything in their own good time. When working, thinking or preparing, Swallows tend to talk to themselves. They are also garrulous in conversation, forever going off at tangents from the topic being discussed. Strangely enough, this can create a sense of shared reverie, having a remarkably calming influence on those who are anxious, worried or under stress. One always has the feeling that somehow everything will work out for the best after a chat with a Swallow friend.

The Swallow Partner

Many born in the Swallow sign are mellow and serene, capable of taking highly-charged or excitable partners in their stride. They exert a pacifying and calming influence on anyone in their vicinity. However, Swallows are unlikely to be happy in close proximity to those who expect others to join them in a world of frenzied activity. They prefer to look, listen and learn, offering pertinent advice or comment at their own time of choosing, rather than be swept away with boundless enthusiasm.

The Swallow lover is romantic and affectionate although sometimes a little too sentimental. They are open and giving and willingly offer their trust. They allow themselves to be captivated by those who bring adventure to their lives, providing it is not too disruptive. For the Swallow to be at their best, they need a stable partner who has a responsible attitude to life. However, for the relationship to be truly successful, their partner must share an imaginative disposition. Moreover, anyone who lacks sensitivity is seldom attractive to those born in the Swallow sign.

Affinity Signs

Cascaya: Many born in the Swallow sign are calm and serene, well able to take the highly-charged Cascayan in their stride.

The Phoenix: The Phoenix gets on best with those who are less active than themselves. Many born in the Swallow sign are calm and serene – at least outwardly. Accordingly, they can exert a positive influence on the Phoenix's impulsive nature.

The Sphinx: The openness of the Swallow is appreciated by the Sphinx and the Swallow is captivated by Sphinx inscrutability. Successful relationships and marriages are highly probable.

The Swallow: The unassuming Swallow is usually happy in the company of other Swallows. They have many common interests, experience few serious disagreements, and share a deep sense of intuition.

The Griffin: The Griffin's strong family ties and protective instincts can make them ideal partners for

Swallows. Swallows often look at life from a very different perspective to the Griffin, and their romantic imagination usually aids the Griffin's creativity.

Problem Signs

The Hero: The Swallow is far too sensitive and emotional for the Hero, while the Hero is too overbearing for the Swallow. The two signs have little in common, and their outlooks on life differ considerably.

Etana: The serenity of life-style the Swallow needs is unlikely to be found in close proximity to the Etana.

The Dragon: The Dragon's energetic mental agility is fascinating, though exhausting, to the peace-loving Swallow.

Other Signs

The Oryx: The Oryx is often attracted to the openness of the Swallow, although the Oryx can mentally exhaust the Swallow who prefers a more serene life-style.

Assari: Swallows and Assaris both share an interest in the exotic and unusual aspects of life. Close friendships and relationships are possible, although marriage between these two signs can sometimes suffer due to a lack of practical considerations.

The Genie: The Genie and Swallow have much in common and can enjoy each other's company. Close friendships and relationships may be problematic due to the Swallow's need for a more assertive partner.

The Serpent: Swallows and Serpents share little in common. However, this can sometimes lead to successful marriages. There is little for them to argue or disagree about.

The Huntress: Swallows are romantics by nature and may find themselves swept away by Huntress panache. The Huntress's life-style is often too dramatic for the Swallow.

Famous Swallows
Jane Seymour. Born: 15 February 1951.

If one word could describe the Swallow woman it would be 'romantic'. Who better to typify this prime Swallow trait than actress Jane Seymour? Her popular roles in historical romance have made her name almost synonymous with the period drama. Swallows so often have that 'still waters run deep' aura, and Jane is no exception. Swallows are the kind of women who seem always to have a secret on their minds, and Jane Seymour seems to personify some eternal feminine mystery.

Ronald Reagan. Born: 6 February 1911.

A Swallow of a very different kind is Ronald Reagan. He may not be a romantic but his approach to the presidency was perhaps the most theatrical of any politician. After all, he was once an actor himself, and many Swallows make dramatic changes of career during the course of their lives. Successful Swallows seldom do anything in the orthodox fashion, and most bring a flamboyant and showy quality to their chosen endeavours. It is hardly surprising that the Reagan years were perhaps the most florid in America's history.

Elizabeth Taylor. Born: 27 February 1932.

The Swallow's need for change and variety is typified by Elizabeth Taylor, whose manifold marriages are almost proverbial. In her varied career she has been a child superstar, a serious Shakespearean actress, a sex symbol, and the epitome of Hollywood high society. Acclaimed for her historical roles, Elizabeth Taylor transported an audience back into a living past. History often has tremendous appeal to Swallows, and many born in this sign bring the past alive through their enthusiasm for bygone times of adventure.

Fate and Fortune

Over the course of the year Swallows can expect the following influences to affect their lives during the separate lunar cycles:

Cascaya: The cool air above the waterfall brings a refreshing change to the flight path of the Swallow. The Cascaya month is a time when problems are lifted for those born in the Swallow sign.

The Phoenix: The firebird offers much excitement to the Swallow's life. Swallows have a deeply romantic temperament; this month brings many opportunities through which romanticism may be channelled.

The Hero: The Hero month can be a time of laborious activity for the Swallow. If lingering problems remain unsolved, this may be the time to act. The Swallow has an especially practical attitude to life during this month, and is well-placed to handle any difficulties that may previously have been avoided.

Assari: The Winged Assari is an imaginative sign. New ideas and intuitive inspiration can open many doors for the Swallow. It is a favourable month for love and romance. Many Swallows meet new partners, get engaged or even married during an Assari month.

The Genie: The Swallow may find this a somewhat difficult month to handle. Combined, the influences of the Genie and Swallow result in unrealistic or impractical enterprises. This is often a period when financial and domestic problems arise, while business affairs may also suffer.

The Griffin: As a treasure guardian, the legendary Griffin is a positive influence for financial matters. It is a month when the Swallow is especially lucky, particularly concerning ventures of chance. Business endeavours initiated at this time are likely to succeed and great reward is possible.

The Oryx: The swift Oryx brings favourable influences to bear on sporting and leisure activities. At social engagements Swallows will be in their element. Positive developments in the course of the Swallow's life could result from new acquaintances made during this month. This is an especially favourable period for love, romance and affairs of the heart.

Etana: The Swallow should be careful not to rush headlong into anything during the cycle of Etana. This month, however, may be an excellent time for the Swallow to take a vacation.

The Serpent: The Serpent is a sign of learning. Any Swallow involved in academic pursuits will find that many ground-breaking achievements result at this time of year. Swallows may find that they are required to learn a new skill in order to obtain the best results from an important enterprise.

The Dragon: During the month of the Dragon, Swallows could experience difficulty in relationships. They will need their own space which others may not be prepared to allow them. The Swallow should stand firm and refuse to be manipulated.

The Sphinx: The Sphinx is the message-bearer for the Swallow. Surprise news is likely in the early days of this month.

The Swallow: The Swallow's own month is a positive influence for change. A move of location or occupation is particularly favourable at this time.

The Huntress: The Huntress month is a time when Swallows appear to have little control over their own affairs. However hard they try they seem to get nowhere. It is often best for Swallows to wait until the Huntress month is over before they make important decisions.

THE HUNTRESS

Intercalary Month

Sign Chart Letter
M

THE HUNTRESS

As the intercalary month, this lunar cycle only occurs every few years. As such, Huntresses are sometimes gifted with rare genius or unique talents. The Huntress in Babylonian mythology was not only a warrior but a spirit of love and adventure. Those born in this sign are therefore both practical and intuitive in their approach to life. Their most incisive attributes arise from a remarkable aptitude to approach problems with an overall perspective. Huntresses can often see things from everyone's point of view.

Huntresses are endowed with an alert and appealing personality. Although outwardly calm and controlled, they harbour a latent wealth of inner emotion. They possess strength of purpose and an innate sense of truth and justice. Fully prepared to admit fault or error, Huntresses have little reticence in changing their ideas or tactics should they be proved wrong. Able to accept warranted criticism as an essential part of learning, most born in this cycle will duly consider the opinions of friends and colleagues in all circumstances.

Huntresses review most situations without personal prejudice, seldom choosing sides in disputes. Such admirable qualities permit those born in this sign to formulate balanced plans and reach level-headed conclusions. The Huntress will patiently look, listen and learn before deciding upon a course of action. Whether or not they agree with others, Huntresses will try to appreciate the validity of all arguments. They are always ready to be persuaded – but reasoning must be sound.

Positive Characteristics

Huntresses share an energetic, attractive and lively personality. A flamboyant character and a flair for the dramatic frequently assures the Huntress centre stage. Confident in most circumstances, the Huntress has a unique talent to gain an overall perspective on any situation. A mystical inclination coupled with a highly developed sense of intuition turns many born in this sign toward philosophical or spiritual pursuits. Huntresses are creative thinkers, having many unique and individual ideas. They are imaginative and adaptable and a popular sense of humour affords them much social success.

Negative Characteristics

Huntresses have a vivid imagination; should problems become too serious they harbour a tendency to retreat into a world of make-believe. Lofty ideas may reduce the chances of success in practical ventures, while unrealistic expectations are a prime source of disappointment for many Huntresses. Wishful thinking is also a danger in business affairs. Sometimes tactless, those born in this sign often speak their mind too readily. Their unconventional views may attract criticism, and a lack of interest in mundane day-to-day concerns can create difficulties in domestic matters. Huntresses apply themselves with total commitment to most endeavours and are sometimes obsessional in their approach.

Appearance

Huntress eyes are wide and expressive. Many born in this sign also have high foreheads and a well-defined widow's peak is not uncommon. They have quick reactions, although most move in a slow or deliberate manner. Everything the Huntress does is undertaken with an appearance of calculated accuracy. Few born in this cycle are likely to sprawl or slouch even when fully relaxed.

Health

The Huntress' intense commitment to projects and endeavours may result in anxiety and other stress-related problems. However, they regulate their lives in such a fashion that they are unlikely to suffer from gastronomical complaints or stomach trouble. One astonishing aspect of the Huntress's physiology is the capacity to heal or recover rapidly from injury. Broken bones mend quickly and cuts and bruises disappear in no time at all.

The Formula for Success

Huntresses are usually honest, forthright and idealistic. Both logic and intuition direct their actions – the perfect blend for success in any undertaking. They are hard-working and blessed with a keen, subtle intelligence, having little difficulty expressing themselves in a clear and eloquent manner. They mix well socially, are easygoing with their acquaintances, are undemanding as friends and helpful as colleagues. Huntresses display imaginative foresight and have the remarkable aptitude to see things from varying perspectives. They will take all angles of a problem into consideration before arriving at conclusions, and are often inspired with revolutionary ideas.

Words of Advice

Idealists by nature, some Huntresses may prefer to live in a world of reverie, even fantasy, if problems become too serious. They may retreat from the dismal, uninviting world and become reserved, secretive and detached. In such circumstances the Huntress must face reality and realize that everything is not always going to work out for the best.

Another Huntress drawback is a tendency toward compulsive devotion to work. For a heart-felt cause, they may devote themselves so entirely that relationships, family life and everyday matters are neglected. Huntresses should be aware of the potentially obsessive side to their character.

Suitable Occupations

A thirst for knowledge draws many born in this sign into academic careers. Equally, an adventurous, enquiring mind suits Huntresses to the world of scientific research. The Huntress has an excellent eye for salient detail, so photography, painting, sculpture, architecture and commercial art are also appealing occupations for many born in this sign. Huntresses enjoy the limelight – whether as orators, performers or professional persuaders, Huntresses accurately gauge public reaction, capture attention and mould opinion with considerable ease. Many successful advertising executives are born in the Huntress sign.

The Huntress at Work

Huntresses have a flexible attitude to work. Their ability to see things from everyone's point of view ideally suits them for positions of responsibility. The Huntress employer is a fair, conscientious and hard-working boss, while the Huntress employee mixes well with colleagues. Few born in the Huntress sign are found entangled in professional squabbles. They make excellent mediators, helping to solve any problems that arise in their place of work.

The Huntress' occupation must offer challenge and scope for initiative. If a job lacks stimulation or creative potential, Huntresses will soon grow bored and lose interest entirely. Until a fulfilling career is found, few Huntresses will remain content with a job for long.

The Huntress Woman

The Huntress woman is born in the most socially versatile of signs. She can converse eruditely at any level, be it at a formal banquet or in her local bar. She possesses a firm set of ideals and, no matter how unconventional they may appear to others, she will defend them with zeal. The Huntress woman insists on being treated on equal terms in male company. Brave is the man who dares to talk down to the Huntress woman or treats her in a chauvinistic manner.

The Huntress woman is a devoted friend, colleague or partner, though she may sometimes seem distant or preoccupied. She may also be changeable in temperament, one minute engrossed in conversation, the next detached in a world of thought. Acquaintances must learn to accept the Huntress the way she is. There is no enmity in her behaviour: out of the blue, an idea completely removed from the current topic may simply have occurred to her.

Both male and female Huntresses often adopt an unconventional style. This is especially true of the Huntress woman. Even if she is a dedicated follower of fashion, or needs to dress formally for work, she will always make an individual statement in her chosen attire. It may be no more than an unusual piece of jewellery, but look closely and somewhere about the Huntress you will find her unique personal trademark.

The Huntress Man

Like the woman of this sign, mental privacy is of utmost importance to the Huntress man, and he will defend it with passion. He may also behave in an unorthodox manner, his motives inscrutable and complex. By contrast, those born in this sign are fascinated by the intentions and motivations of others. Be they friends, lovers or mere acquaintances, Huntresses are determined to discover just what it is that makes people tick. The Huntress man therefore has a paradoxical, enigmatic personality that many women find enchanting.

The Huntress male is usually attracted to women who lead interesting or exotic lives. At the very least they must share an unusual approach to life. To his partner he is kind and generous, but his lover must accept that, like his female counterpart, he will insist upon his own personal space. In this respect the Huntress shares much in common with the Genie – they just hate invasion of their private thoughts and contemplations. However, Huntresses seldom have anything to hide, they simply need to retreat from time to time. Mental solitude often enables them to solve not only their own problems but also those of others.

The Huntress Parent

Huntress parents will encourage their children to think for themselves and stand on their own two feet. They bring banal school subjects to life by injecting flair and imagination, making learning a more stimulating activity. Few Huntresses insist that their children adopt their own interests and values, neither will they reprimand their young without a fair hearing. Both

Huntress mothers and fathers alike will listen to their children eagerly and with an open mind before passing judgement on their motives or actions.

The Huntress Child

Right from infancy Huntress children are dreamers, their ambitions high and their hearts overflowing with expectation. An observant intelligence combined with extraordinary intuition often results in 'an old head on young shoulders'. Huntress children are constantly questioning the world about them, not satisfied until they have discovered the answer for everything that grabs their attention. Consequently, the young Huntress may lack concentration in school, gazing through the classroom window at something more exciting outside. When they apply themselves, however, they are immensely creative achievers. Physical activity is not high on their list of priorities, even if they do have the physique to excel at sport. The Huntress child much prefers to work alone rather than as part of an organized group or team.

The Huntress Friend

Huntresses are their own people, refusing to be drawn into any type of close-knit or elite community. They dislike conformity, preferring to remain an elusive but prominent figure in the crowd. Huntresses enjoy socializing – they can be extremely witty, humorous and fun-loving – but hate to confine themselves to one set of standards or principles. Everything has its place in Huntress philosophy, and everyone has the right to their own opinions and life-style. Anyone who is dogmatic, inflexible or stuck in a rut is unlikely to be a Huntress' friend. More than anything else, Huntresses despise prejudice or injustice of any kind.

Huntresses often experience difficulty in making long-term friends, despite their engaging and magnetic personalities. They are usually so different from others that they find it impossible to share continual enthusiasm for the same old routines. Once they do meet someone with whom they share a common outlook, Huntresses can cast an irresistible spell on their new-found friend, leading them into a world of wonder and excitement. Furthermore, Huntresses will do all in their power to protect those they love, sacrificing themselves should the need arise.

The Huntress Partner

Young Huntresses often share unrealistic expectations of their chosen partners and, more often than not, will encounter disappointment. Eventually their attitude will adapt itself to harsh reality and a compromise will be reached. Once committed, the Huntress will be a devoted and passionate lover, although public displays of affection are rare. Successful marriages are possible so long as the Huntress' partner allows the Huntress to retain their individualism and personal freedom. The Huntress is averse to interference in their affairs, no matter who by or how well-intended.

Occasionally Huntresses will seek temporary escape from the world to become at one with themselves. At such times they will retreat and contemplate in solitude. Partners may sometimes take this the wrong way, mistakenly believing that they have done something to offend. Provided they are left to sort out their problems alone, Huntresses will soon return contented.

Affinity Signs

The Phoenix: In legend, once reborn, the Phoenix was impelled to fly to the temple of Heliopolis. Like the mythical bird, those born in the Phoenix sign will find themselves attracted to the exotic or unusual. The Huntress is perhaps the most intriguing of signs, and their idiosyncratic style is irresistible to the Phoenix.

Assari: Assaris are often attracted to the unconventional Huntress, while Huntresses move towards those with imagination. These signs are most compatible, and many successful marriages and business partnerships result.

The Serpent: The Serpent's love of learning is much respected by the Huntress. The Serpent finds the Huntress' unique insight equally fascinating. The two signs work well together and marriages are often successful.

The Dragon: Huntresses can take the energetic Dragon in their stride. Dragons often need a benevolent and controlling hand which the Huntress is prepared to offer. Almost all the attributes lacking in one sign are compensated by the other, and some of the most successful marriages are formed between Huntresses and Dragons.

Problem Signs

Cascaya: Huntresses need their own space. The Cascayan intends to be a part of everything too much for the Huntress' liking.

The Huntress: Few Huntresses feel at ease in the company of others who share their sign. The Huntress' life is often too unusual to be spent so close to another who has similarly unconventional attitudes.

The Genie: Huntresses tend to fall for Genii, although Genies may find the Huntress way of living somewhat insecure for their liking.

Other Signs

The Oryx: Although the Huntress and the Oryx mix well socially, relationships or business partnerships can suffer. When together, they tend to behave irresponsibly.

The Hero: The Hero admires the resourceful Huntress, but the Huntress often finds the Hero far too conventional in their approach to life.

Etana: As both Etanas and Huntresses commit themselves so completely to a chosen pursuit, these two signs work well together if they share a similar heartfelt interest. If their interests lie in different directions, however, they are unlikely to have the time to spare for one another.

The Sphinx: The Huntress is a sign that can solve the Sphinx's eternal riddle. Huntress intuition gives them the ability to fathom the motives of those born in the cycle of the Sphinx. The Sphinx may find this acutely unnerving.

The Swallow: Swallows are romantics by nature and may find themselves swept away by Huntress panache. The Huntress' life-style is often too dramatic for the Swallow.

The Griffin: The Huntress can unnerve the Griffin. Few Griffins like ideas as unconventional as those many Huntresses appear to share.

Famous Huntresses

Mikhail Gorbachev. Born: 2 March 1931.

Only occurring every few years, the Huntress is often a sign of rare or revolutionary achievements. As Soviet president, Mikhail Gorbachev single-handedly changed the face of world politics. Huntresses have a firm grasp of complex matters which often confuse those born in other signs. The Huntress' ability to assimilate complicated information and to re-present it in a lucid and compelling manner made President Gorbachev the most competent player on the Russian political scene. The Huntress is one of the most imaginative signs, and Mikhail Gorbachev, both supporters and opponents agreed, was one of the most imaginative politicians of his time. A radical change of direction is usual once a Huntress takes the reigns of any endeavour.

George Harrison. Born: 25 February 1943.

Many Huntresses are inclined towards the mystical or sublime. Typical in this respect is George Harrison who has made no secret of his profound interest in eastern mysticism. The Huntress is also a sign of benevolence, and many born in this cycle will spend much time and effort helping those who are less fortunate than themselves. George Harrison is forever at the forefront of charitable fund-raising and famine relief, and is a leading figure in many activities to help the developing world.

Drew Barrymore. Born: 22 February 1975.

Actress Drew Barrymore has enjoyed a prolific career. Typical Huntress, she possesses a complex array of characteristics consistent with this unusual sign. With magnetic appeal and a flamboyant personality, she has become a one-of-a-kind enigma on the Hollywood scene. Like many born in the Huntress sign, she insists on her personal space, and will sometimes retreat from the limelight. Many Huntresses have a unique, almost magical appeal and, as such, Drew Barrymore has attracted an almost cult-like following across the world.

Fate and Fortune

Over the course of the year Huntresses can expect the following influences to affect their lives during the separate lunar cycles:

Cascaya: The month of Cascaya is a time for the Huntress to plan. Any idea formulated during this cycle should lead to success. The influences of the intangible Cascaya can easily be directed and channelled by the celestial Huntress. Any Huntress seeking a new romantic relationship, could find this month particularly favourable.

The Phoenix: During the Phoenix month the Huntress often experiences greatest difficulty. Huntresses prefer one thing to end before another begins. Something the Huntress considered over and done with may return. An unwelcome connection with the past could open old wounds.

The Hero: The Hero and the Huntress work hand-in-hand to ensure success. This is a month when hard work can finally pay off. The Hero is also the message-bearer for the Huntress, and surprise news is likely toward the end of this cycle.

Assari: The winged Assari can fly the Huntress to exotic locations. This is the month when travel is favourable. Any Huntress seeking change of home or occupation may discover new opportunities.

The Genie: The month of the Genie is a time of re-flection and contemplation for the Huntress. Outstanding problems may be resolved through Hun-tress intuition. A new acquaintance may alter the course of the Huntress' life. This is an especially favourable month for love, romance and affairs of the heart.

The Griffin: To the Huntress the Griffin will relinquish its treasure. This month is favourable for anything con-cerning finance, and good fortune around the end of this cycle is likely.

The Oryx: The rare Oryx can be tracked and captured by the wiles of the Huntress. This is a particularly favourable period for romantic affairs. Many Hun-tresses first meet their future partners during the Oryx month. In business the Oryx brings new opportunities for prosperity.

Etana: Domestic matters are likely to play an important role in the life of the Huntress during this cycle, and the home may need more attention than usual. This is a month of good luck concerning ventures of chance.

The Serpent: During the month of the Serpent

Huntresses could find themselves inadvertently drawn into problems over which they have no control.

The Dragon: The energetic Dragon positively influences the Huntress. A particularly favourable time for sport and leisure activities. Huntresses engaged in competition are especially likely to fare well.

The Sphinx: During the month of the Sphinx the Huntress may acquire something which has been long sought, only to discover it is not as they expected.

The Swallow: The Swallow brings social success for the Huntress. If Huntresses attend parties or a special occasion during this month they could be in for a pleasant surprise.

The Huntress: During their own month Huntresses are often inspired by unique and original ideas. Projects initiated during this cycle have far-reaching consequences. A complete change of life-style may be initiated.

SELECT BIBLIOGRAPHY

Dalley, S. *Myths from Mesopotamia*, Oxford 1989

Day, M. S. *The Many Meanings of Myth*, London 1984

Gadd, C. J. *The Stones of Assyria*, London 1936

Grant, M. *Roman Myths*, London 1971

Graves, R. *The Greek Myths*, Harmondsworth 1955

Grayson, A. K. *Assyrian and Babylonian Chronicles*, New York 1975

Hooke, S. H. *Babylonian and Assyrian Religion*, London 1953

James, O. E. *Myth and Ritual*, London 1958

Laessoe, J. *People of Ancient Assyria*, London 1963

Lambert, W. G. *Babylonian Wisdom Literature*, Oxford 1960

Luckenbill, D. D. *Ancient Records of Assyria and Babylonia: Vol I*, Chicago 1926

Luckenbill, D. D. *Ancient Records of Assyria and Babylonia: Vol II*, Chicago 1926

McCall, H. *Mesopotamia Myths*, London 1990

Mallowan, M. E. L. *Nimrud and its Remains: Vol I*, London 1966

Mallowan, M. E. L. *Nimrud and its Remains: Vol II*, London 1966

Moortgat, A. *The Art of Ancient Mesopotamia*, London 1969

Oates, J. *Babylon*, London 1979

Oppenheim, A. L. *Ancient Mesopotamia: Portrait of a Dead Civilization*, Chicago 1964

Saggs, H. W. F. *The Might that was Assyria*, London 1984

Saggs, H. W. F. *Everyday Life in Babylonia and Assyria*, London 1987

Saggs, H. W. F. *The Greatness that was Babylon*, London 1988

Thompson, R. C. *The Reports of the Magicians and Astrologers of Nineveh and Babylon: Vol I*, London 1900

Thompson, R. C. *The Reports of the Magicians and Astrologers of Nineveh and Babylon: Vol II*, London 1900

Thompson, R. C. *The Epic of Gilgamesh*, Oxford 1930

Waerden, B. L. *The Birth of Astronomy*, Oxford 1974

Wilson, J. V. K. *The Legend of Etana*, Warminster 1985